Gamal Abdel Nasser
A Bibliography

Gamal Abdel Nasser

A Bibliography

Faysal Mikdadi

**BIBLIOGRAPHIES OF
WORLD LEADERS, NO. 5**

GREGORY PALMER, SERIES EDITOR

GREENWOOD PRESS
New York • Westport, Connecticut • London

Library of Congress Cataloging-in-Publication Data

Mikdadi, F. H.
  Gamal Abdel Nasser : a bibliography / Faysal Mikdadi.
    p.   cm.—(Bibliographies of world leaders, ISSN 1056–5523 ; no. 5)
  Includes indexes.
  ISBN 0–313–28119–X (alk. paper)
  1. Nasser, Gamal Abdel, 1918–1970—Bibliography. I. Title.
II. Series.
Z8614.74.M54   1991
[DT107.83]
016.96205′3′092—dc20   91–21168

British Library Cataloguing in Publication Data is available.

Library of Congress Catalog Card Number: 91–21168
ISBN: 0–313–28119–X
ISSN: 1056–5523

First published in 1991

Greenwood Press, 88 Post Road West, Westport, CT 06881
An imprint of Greenwood Publishing Group, Inc.

Printed in the United States of America

The paper used in this book complies with the
Permanent Paper Standard issued by the National
Information Standards Organization (Z39.48–1984).

10 9 8 7 6 5 4 3 2 1

Contents

Preface

This bibliography aims to provide a comprehensive set of references to Nasser's life, including his writings and major speeches. Nasser's historical importance lies in his Pan-Arab policies, his transformation of Egypt from a feudal British Protectorate to a modern industrial nation and his contribution to third world politics.

This bibliography is designed for American and British readers. In a few cases it includes French, Arabic, German and other works. Where a translation or summary in English is available reference is made to it. Titles in languages other than English are, therefore, followed by an English translation in brackets. Arabic names and titles have been transliterated into English script using the most common Western spellings where known personalities are involved.

The biographical section aims to give as full a background to Nasser as is possible within the space available. Largely because Nasser's influence was also due to his legendary charisma in the Arab world, an attempt has been made to analyse his personality and to convey the atmosphere engendered during his leadership.

Acknowledgements

Compiling a bibliography risks being a very lonely business. My main thanks for making it much less so go to my wife, Susan, and my children, Catherine and Richard. Their help and patience made the work a labour of love. Equally my thanks go to my colleagues Jacinta Hegarty, David Martin and David Pert for similar help and encouragement.

I also wish to thank the following for their kind comments and constructive criticisms of the Summary Biography of Nasser and the Chronology of the Life of Gamal Abdel Nasser: Michael Adams, Stuart Macwilliam, The Lord Mayhew, Christine Middleton, Michael Middleton and The Rt. Hon. Sir Anthony Nutting, Bart.

Acknowledgments are also due to the following for facilitating my research at their respective institutions: Stuart Macwilliam, Assistant Librarian at the University of Exeter Library, Stephen L. Roberts, Centre Director of the Reference Centre of the United States Information Service and Susan Taylor of the Wiltshire Library and Museum Service.

I also received grateful assistance from personnel at the British Library, The Egyptian Cultural Attaché's Office and the Egyptian Maktab al-A'llam, the Public Records Office, the Swindon Central Library and the University of Essex Library.

Finally, it would be difficult to describe my gratitude to my editor Greg Palmer for his advice, encouragement, trust and patience.

The portrait of the late President Nasser appears with the permission of Constable Publishers from their publication *Nasser* by Anthony Nutting.

Gamal Abdel Nasser. Used with permission from Anthony Nutting. *Nasser*.
London: Constable Publishers.

Summary Biography of Nasser

Youth and Rise to Power

Nasser was born into an Egypt stricken with poverty and "in a state of hopeless despair" as he once put it to an adolescent friend. For two and a half thousand years the Egyptians had lived under foreign domination. As an adolescent Nasser became widely read in philosophy and literature. He became a firm believer in the importance of dignity in national affairs, a belief that became his guiding light all through his life. As a fervent Egyptian nationalist, he wanted to see the British out of Egypt with Egyptian independence creating that "dignity" necessary for the Egyptians to run their own affairs.

Nasser grew up in an atmosphere of resurgent Egyptian nationalism. The Wafdist Party Prime Minister Nahas signed a treaty in 1936 with the British giving nominal sovereignty to Egypt whilst maintaining a strong British military presence in the Suez. Such a treaty suited King Farouk of Egypt whose unpopularity led him to rely heavily on British protection.

During the serious situation in the North African campaign in the Second World War, Britain exacted a humiliating surrender of national sovereignty from King Farouk. The King had been hesitating in his dealings with the British since he saw an ally against them in the Germans. The mass demonstrations following the 1936 treaty made him realise the necessity of ridding Egypt of the British. The British, however, were suffering setbacks at the hands of Rommel. In a virtual state of panic the British Ambassador used the military to extract from the King an Egyptian government more sympathetic to the British cause. Nahas, the architect of the 1936 treaty, was then appointed Prime Minister. From then onwards Farouk's days were numbered.

Nasser's heavy involvement in the 1936 demonstrations and his humble origins made it difficult for him to join the Military Academy or the Police Academy. A year later, with the gall that was to mark many of his later acts, Nasser visited the minister responsible and appealed to be admitted into the Military Academy. After his graduation he volunteered for service in the Sudan.

Nahas's Wafd government and King Farouk became symbols of British domination. After Farouk's capitulation to the British military threat, Nasser and his fellow officers formed a group dedicated to gaining for Egypt independence from British control. Soon this group became known as the Free Officers' movement: fervently nationalist and in search of that "dignity" which had eluded Egypt and by which Nasser set such store all through his life.

At this stage it was still felt that King Farouk, as a symbol of Egyptian nationhood, was there to stay. The Free Officers, though politically aware, were not ambitious for power. Theirs was a vague ambition for an Egypt without Britain. But events were to overtake them.

With the signing of the Bevin Sidky Protocol, Britain was to leave Egypt by 1949 in return for a defence pact allowing for her return in case of an attack on Egypt or any neighbouring country. The agreement also allowed Egyptian sovereignty over the Sudan. Sudanese and British popular clamour against the treaty caused its almost immediate collapse and the fall of the Nahas government.

To add to Egypt's mounting problems, with the Israeli declaration of independence after the UN partition of Palestine, the Egyptians became embroiled in the first Arab-Israeli war of 1948–49. It was during this period that Nasser and his group of Free Officers became thoroughly politicised with designs leading to outright revolution. Nasser himself, as well as subsequent biographers, saw this period as having a profound influence on his thinking.

Nasser, by now promoted to Captain, became trapped in the famous Falluja siege. His first contacts with the Israelis date to that time when he refused to surrender despite his troops' hopeless position. He eventually led a counter offensive that allowed his men to hold out until the armistice some five months later.

Although a war hero, Nasser was profoundly upset and shaken by his country's experience of this war. He saw the widespread corruption that resulted in the defective armoury delivered to troops. The King and his palace clique were making fortunes out of the war and, as Nasser saw it, out of the soldier's misery and suffering.

On an international level, Nasser saw Israel as the recipient of decisive military support whilst Egypt received none. He also saw the inadequacy of Arab intentions and their disunity against Israel's unity of purpose and European technology.

It became evident to Nasser that Arab unity was the only way to defeat the alien Western culture of Israel sapping at the heart of the Moslem-Arab world. He also realised that Egypt had to rid itself not only of Britain but also of King Farouk and the bourgeoisie that exploited the ordinary Egyptian. Furthermore, he felt that the ordinary Egyptian had to be taught to govern himself or herself and to obtain his or her own national dignity.

By 1952, the corruption prevalent in Egypt was also traced to the Prime Minister whose wife was involved in dubious and illegal business dealings. The returned Nahas, meanwhile, having failed to reach an agreement with the British the year before, abrogated the 1936 treaty. Coupled with this was the launching of a guerrilla campaign by the Moslem Brotherhood against the British.

The British response was swift and fierce. Riots against the British were suppressed. The Free Officers found themselves having to speed up their plans. Finally, with the police and the palace about to arrest them, they struck on the night of July 23, 1952.

In a bloodless coup with classic deployment of troops, King Farouk was forced to abdicate and leave the country with a considerable amount of the treasury with him. At this juncture we have another illuminating insight into Nasser's character. He had opposed his colleagues' demand to kill the palace clique. Now, as his colleagues demanded that Farouk be attacked in international waters in order to retrieve the treasury haul, Nasser opposed them. He had a horror of bloodletting since an abortive assassination attempt a few years before.

Colonel Nasser became the de facto ruler of Egypt in all but name. General Neguib, more known than any of the Free Officers, was made titular Head of State for a while. After some internal wranglings over policy and application, Neguib was put under house arrest, and Nasser took over the functions of the Presidency.

The character formed over the previous thirty four years was one that had a fervent belief in personal dignity, Egyptian nationalism, Arab unity, a strong suspicion of, and yet pragmatically begrudging admiration for, the West, a belief in justice, a wide knowledge of philosophy and some literature, a puritanical approach to daily life and a heavy reliance on smoking. These characteristics were coupled with the qualities of insularity of thought, a tendency to forgive too easily, a fierce loyalty to friends and allies, a naïveté in largely believing others, belief in the best in everyone coupled with a duplicity in handling antagonists and fortuitous suspicion of successful colleagues and a theatricality of action that made many of his decisions seem beyond or outside apparent political reality.

Thus, with a mixture of bitter experience and charming naïveté Nasser was set to govern Egypt for the next eighteen turbulent years.

Approaches to the West

With Egypt rid of its King, Nasser and his Revolutionary Command Council (RCC) set out to reform the country. Land was distributed to the enfranchised Egyptian peasant. Other social and educational reforms were set in motion. The old army command was replaced by new blood and an attempt was made to strengthen it.

In order to do all of this and to deal with the dire state of Egypt's economy, Nasser needed the financial backing necessary to purchase the technological wherewithal and expertise. He could not turn to the Russians because, as a Moslem, he felt a strong antipathy towards Communism whose adherents were being suppressed in Egypt. Despite earlier experiences of Western imperialism, he felt more comfortable in approaching the West particularly the Americans for whom he had a great admiration.

Initial contacts with Kermit Roosevelt of the CIA and William Foster, Assistant Secretary of State for Defence, were successful. Nasser's relaxed dealings coupled with his sense of humour seemed to have inveigled his visitors to promise major trade agreements. Britain vetoed this when it became apparent that she was not going to succeed in getting Nasser to agree to her terms for withdrawal from Egypt. At Nasser's insistence, however, Egypt dropped any claim of sovereignty over the Sudan.

With Britain's persistence over her right to remain in Egypt to safeguard her interest in Suez, the pre-revolution war of attrition against her forces was resumed. Meanwhile President Eisenhower made it clear that the United States would supply massive aid to Egypt as soon as the latter reached an agreement with Britain.

An agreement was soon reached allowing for imminent British withdrawal in return for a temporary sharing of Suez military establishments. Egypt also promised to uphold the principle of freedom of navigation through Suez enshrined in the 1888 Constantinople Convention.

However, the Americans were not yet ready to deliver on their promises except with a small economic assistance package. With the cold war intensifying, Britain proposed a defence alliance including Britain, Iraq, Turkey and Pakistan. The Baghdad Pact was immediately seen as a threat by Nasser. Britain, about to lose its foothold in Egypt, was re-entering the Arab arena through the Iraqi backdoor. Furthermore, with Britain's membership to NATO and Iraq's membership to the Arab League Egypt might have found itself drawn into conflicts of Britain's making. The latter's recent imperialist history did not augur well for Britain's peaceful intentions. Nasser saw the Baghdad Pact as yet another attempt to treat the Arabs as a subject race devoid of dignity or independence.

Nasser's frantic attempts to persuade the Iraqis against joining the Pact failed miserably. The Arab League members were woefully divided: Jordan's King Hussein relied entirely on the British to run and maintain his army, Lebanon's President Chamoun was occidental to his fingertips, the Syrians were under their eleventh government in less than three years. The Saudis were economically and logistically pro-Western and so on with every member state.

Nasser's only response to the Baghdad Pact was to launch vituperative attacks on the Iraqis through the Voice of the Arabs radio station. These attacks were soon to embrace all countries or persons perceived to be anti-Arab, e.g., Nuri of Iraq, Chamoun of Lebanon, the Syrian régime and, later on, the Jordanians. These broadcasts were later to be followed by incitements to local opposition groups to topple their pro-Western governments.

As Nasser continued to woo the Americans for aid another blow was struck at Egypt from another pro-Western nation. Nasser had maintained secret contacts with Israeli Premier Sharett with the hope of establishing a permanent peace equitable both to the Palestinians and the Israelis. He was pragmatic enough to know that Israel was there to stay. The question was on the form that an Israeli-Palestinian settlement should take. All attempts to resolve this issue were to prove unsuccessful.

With an Israeli attack against Egyptian army headquarters in Gaza came a lengthy war of attrition. For every guerrilla attack launched from Gaza Israel retaliated on an increasingly large scale. These attacks were to prove disastrous in forming Nasser's domestic and foreign policies.

After the first Gaza raid, Nasser found himself under intolerable pressure to acquire the arms necessary for the defence of Egypt against Israel. He also resolved to strengthen the defence capabilities of the Arab League. Meanwhile, he re-instituted the guerrilla attacks against Israeli territory and increased his propaganda campaign against Iraq in order to foment local rebellion against King Faysal and his henchman Nuri.

With Western military supplies to Israel increased by a large shipment of French jet fighters, Nasser turned to the West again. Faced with Western conditions that he could not possibly keep, he reluctantly turned to Russia. Even as a Russo-Egyptian agreement was about to be signed, Nasser tried a last attempt to obtain arms from Britain and the United States but to no avail.

One year before Suez and with Israeli raids increasing, President Nasser turned to the Soviet Union for large arms deals and commercial agreements.

Suez

Having failed to reach an accommodation over the Sudan question which eventually led to complete independence, Nasser resorted to outright bribery in an effort to woo the Sudanese to some sort of link with Egyptian sovereignty. These efforts, coupled with behind the scenes double dealings by the British, caused the first major animosity between Nasser and Eden. Egypt's arms deal with the Soviet Union deepened Eden's resolve to topple Nasser as the man most threatening to Britain's Middle East interests.

Between 1955 and 1956 Egypt tried, with some apparent initial success, to procure massive Western loans for building the Aswan High Dam. Apart from the Dam's apparent use in increasing irrigation in a country whose population was increasing too rapidly, the Aswan project took on exaggerated dimensions relating to Egypt's national pride and independence.

Both Britain and the United States attached impossible conditions to their loans which Nasser interpreted as a form of economic imperialism. Whilst these negotiations were taking place, Jordan seemed about to join the infamous Baghdad Pact. Under intense local pressure, King Hussein of Jordan dismissed Glubb Pasha, his British army commander. Soon after that Nasser recognised Communist China in an attempt to procure further arms from the Eastern bloc. Britain saw both actions as hostile to her and Eden's suspicions of Nasser increased to an almost personal paranoia. He was joined in this by Dulles of the United States and the French premier Mollet smarting from the Algerian rebellion. The latter supplied Israel with modern weapons. Egyptian suspicion of the French increased when French forces hijacked the Algerian leader's plane and promptly arrested him despite having guaranteed him safe conduct beforehand.

Even at this late stage, the Americans tried their hand at a peace initiative. Dulles' envoy, Anderson, failed to convince Nasser to enter into direct negotiation with Israel. Ben Gurion's insistence on nothing less than direct talks made the American mission a failure before it had even started.

By 1956 relations between Egypt and the West were at a very low ebb. Britain and the United States reneged on their promises to support the Aswan High Dam.

Nasser, still unwilling to accept Russian offers of help, decided to raise the foreign currency revenue necessary for the project by nationalising the Suez Canal.

Whilst Eden was discussing with some Americans the possibility of a coup d'état to bring the Egyptian government down, Nasser delivered his famous coup during a speech carefully outlining a step by step Egyptian perception of Western treachery. The Canal was nationalised. This was to be the biggest gamble of Nasser's career and it paid off.

No sooner had the Suez Canal been taken over by the Egyptians than the British set in motion a series of attempts calculated to pressure Nasser into recanting on his decision. Britain called up reservists into the army as an initial gesture whilst Eden lost no opportunity in publicly denouncing Nasser. Further attempts to douse international political emotions were all doomed to failure as Nasser insisted on Egypt's right under international law to run the Canal. Despite the Canal Company's attempts to sabotage Egyptian efforts, the Canal was kept open and its use actually increased during that period of intense political activity.

As further negotiations took place, France, Israel and Britain laid their plans to capture Suez. Israel was to launch an attack. Britain and France were to issue an ultimatum to belligerents telling them to cease hostilities and to withdraw their forces ten miles either side of the Canal thus allowing Anglo-French forces to place themselves in between. In essence this meant that Israel was to advance to ten miles from the Canal while Egypt was to withdraw from Gaza and the Sinai to ten miles from the western bank of the Canal.

As events unfolded, General Abdel Hakim Amer, thrown into a state of panic, urged Nasser to accept the ultimatum. Nasser refused. The next few days were to be decisive in forming his future political career.

As the British launched their air attack and as their troops, accompanied by the French, landed in Port Said, Nasser issued arms to the Egyptian people for a guerrilla war. When Egypt's radio transmitters were knocked out, Nasser took to the streets to bolster his compatriots' will to resist. He used the Azhar mosque to deliver his exhortations in a way reminiscent of early Islamic leaders.

With Amer forgetting to issue the necessary orders to his men to wage guerrilla warfare, Port Said fell to Anglo-French forces. The Russians made a great deal of noise but, preoccupied with their own problems in Hungary, they did nothing to rally to Egypt's support.

President Eisenhower stepped in to ensure that the UN General Assembly's vote against the tripartite invasion should be carried out. Under intense American pressure the French and the British withdrew before the end of the year followed by the Israelis a few months later.

The Suez War meant four things in terms of Nasser's future development. Firstly, his success in scuttling the tripartite invasion placed him at the pinnacle of his popularity with the Arab world in particular and with the third world in general. To most Arabs he became their natural leader and to many he was almost deified. This meant that other Arab leaders had to bear in mind his popularity amongst their own people in all their dealings. Even the disastrous defeat suffered by the Egyptians at the hand of the Israelis in 1967 did not detract from his unparalleled popularity. Secondly, with the British out of the Middle East and their Empire crumbling as third world countries sought to emulate Egypt, the United States and Russia came face to face in the Arab world. Thirdly, Nasser's constant assertion of the West's neo-colonialist aims were proved all too true by the apparent crass stupidity of the British and the French throwing their lot in with Israel in a conspiracy the echoes of which lived on for years to come. The latter's expansionist aims became a byword of Arab nationalism and solidarity. Suez thus launched Nasser on his pan-Arab adventures. Finally, Nasser's fierce loyalty to his friends and his tendency to forgive were proved all too true a weakness. General Amer, found woefully wanting in his command, was quickly forgiven by Nasser. This quality of mercy was a fatal personal and political error, for ten years later it was Amer's incompetence and cowardice which helped Israel's sensational and victorious blitzkrieg against Egypt's armed forces.

Non-Alignment

Nasser's economic reliance on Russian aid and easy credit was as worrying to him as Western colonialism. He tried to preserve some form of economic neutrality by working with the Indian, Japanese and West German markets.

Britain's departure from the Middle East left a gap that the United States attempted to fill. This was repugnant to Nasser's perception of his people's nationhood. It was felt that Britain's departure had not actually left a gap as Western analysts would claim. How could a gap exist when Egypt had filled it for thousands of years? The theory of superpower gaps was essentially colonialist since the West saw the rest of the world as being made up of spheres of influence peopled by subject races. This essentially patronizing orientalist approach was unacceptable to Nasser and others like him. Such like-minded persons were to join forces with him to form the Non-aligned movement.

Nasser, Tito of Yugoslavia and Nehru of India met at the Bandung Conference. The three developed a close personal friendship which led to a political alliance. Theirs was to be a neutralist position seeking to influence the superpowers in achieving world peace. This position became known as positive neutralism to its detractors. The three leaders preferred to call it Non-alignment.

Non-alignment could be seen in two lights. At best it was an innocuous concept of neutrality in world affairs. At worst it was the moral cowardice of leaders unable or unwilling to make a stand on important international political questions.

Nasser, Tito and Nehru saw Non-alignment as a potent third force. The world was made up of two massive camps. One, led by the United States, included the Western powers. The other was led by the U.S.S.R. and included all the Communist states. Nasser saw both camps vying with each other in achieving neo-colonialist spheres of influence. Non-alignment was the third camp that wished to remain free of outside control whilst maintaining a restraining influence on the two superpowers. Non-aligned nations strove to solve political problems supposedly on their merits and without reference to the superpowers' cold war.

Tito saw Non-alignment as the very basis of Yugoslavia's existence. During the Yalta conference Roosevelt, Churchill and Stalin had carved up the world into spheres of influence. From Tito's point of view this decision meant that Yugoslavia became part of Russia's sphere. Consequently, Yugoslavia's national aspirations took second place to Russia's dictates. Tito's political genius was shown in his ability to steer Yugoslav independence and integrity within the tightly held Stalinist grip.

To Nehru, Non-alignment meant that, as he put it, "for the first time in history, the least powerful [were] making demands on the most powerful."

A neutral Egypt was not a new concept. As far back as the days of the

Nationalist Party, there was talk of neutrality. By the time Nasser came on the scene Egypt needed not only political independence but also the economic independence that he felt would imbue the Egyptian with a sense of dignity and nationhood.

By the time the second Non-aligned conference was held in Cairo in 1964 it had become clear that the movement was a failure. There were several reasons for this.

The superpowers regarded the Non-aligned movement with deep suspicion. Both the United States and Russia did not miss an opportunity to torpedo its aspirations. To many Americans Non-alignment meant that those nations were against American interests. When the first Non-aligned conference took place in Belgrade in 1961, the Russians announced their intention to resume nuclear weapons testing. This announcement was calculated to nullify any efforts made by the Non-aligned nations to temper superpower aggression. It worked as a ploy thus throwing the conference into turmoil.

Non-alignment was more a concept than a reality. Nasser described it as "not a state [but] a trend." As such, Non-alignment did not have the political or military clout to make itself felt on the world stage.

Furthermore, it was difficult to be neutral when countries like Egypt desperately needed economic and military aid from any quarter willing to provide it. Nasser's foreign policy of Non-alignment was seen by many as the Egyptian leader playing a game where, according to Middle East veteran Copeland, "the strategy of the weak player [was] to play off the strong players against one another . . . and if a single weak player [could] do this to good effect, a 'union' of weak players [could] do it to better effect." To a large extent, that was exactly what Nasser did—at times with outstanding success.

In Egyptian terms, Non-alignment also took on the fight against neo-colonialism as a means of liberating nations from superpower dominance. The result was Nasser's heavy involvement in liberation movements all across Africa, Asia and the Middle East. Such support was bound to anger the superpowers whose spheres of influence policies were being scuttled. It also meant that Nasser was seen as supporting largely left-wing causes against the free world, therefore how could he claim to be non-aligned? Non-alignment became a movement that seemed to have a distinct anti-Western bias despite Nasser's insistence that it was basically about positive neutralism rather than about negative hostility towards any nation. These sentiments seemed largely belied by the endless series of Western press photographs of Nasser in the company of Che Guevara,

Castro, Krushchev, Chou En Lai, Tito, Kosygin, Brezhnev, Ben Bella, Aref and many other reputedly undemocratic Marxist leaders.

Events also overtook the Non-aligned movement. When, in a border dispute, China attacked India in 1962, Non-alignment's weakness was revealed. Both China and India had been at the Bandung conference. China supposedly subscribed to the ideals of Afro-Asian independence outlined at the conference. Yet the Chinese attack on India was launched on the road from Sinkiang which was actually being built immediately after the Bandung conference. This indicated that the Chinese had already decided to wrest Indian territory by force at the very time that they were paying lip service to the higher ideals of the conference. Chou En Lai felt that Non-alignment, at the time strongly supported by the Soviet Union, was becoming a threat to Chinese foreign policy then at odds with Russia. With most Non-aligned nations refusing to take sides in a war involving one of their members (India) and another of the Bandung group (China), the movement was discredited in the eyes of many Indians. Nehru's foreign policy became difficult to justify. The Sino-Indian conflict was one from which he never fully recovered. During that period, Nasser tried to mediate and ultimately played some role in bringing about peace. However, despite his modest success, his Non-aligned stand was seen by many, especially in India, as a betrayal of a fellow Non-aligned nation. The few Non-aligned nations that did condemn China were essentially pro-Western in sympathy which only led to the further disintegration of the movement.

Non-alignment was probably a commendable philosophy towards world peace. Its adherents such as Nasser, Tito and Nehru were certainly sincere in their views. However, they had to walk a tightrope between putting idealism into practice whilst maintaining two realistic approaches. One was the practical need for economic and military aid thus causing the spirit of Non-alignment to have its hands firmly tied. The other was what Nasser was to call, with characteristic honesty, his "reaction to events" policy. In Non-alignment as well as in many other areas of Nasser's foreign policy, he often found himself reacting to events beyond his control. Such was the state of Egyptian foreign policy in the Arab world.

Pan-Arabism

Nasser emerged from Suez as the undisputed leader of Arab nationalism. The euphoria that followed his heady diplomatic and political triumphs made him the acclaimed leader of most non-Egyptian Arabs. This adulation was bound to make other Arab leaders regard him with the utmost suspicion as a usurper of their political powers and local prestige.

In the years that followed, Nasser dealt with internecine Arab feuding within a framework of kitchen sink politics coupled with a theatricality that sometimes made it difficult to separate aspirations from political realities. Having also been declared diabetic, Nasser's health deteriorated progressively over the coming years. He dealt with fellow Arabs with a mixture of knee-jerk reactions and strong kitchen sink approaches. Such dealings smacked of the intense and trivial emotionalism and sentimentality seen in squabbling families.

Nasser's first quarrel was with King Hussein of Jordan. The Voice of the Arabs launched vituperative attacks on the King who responded by aligning himself with King Faysal of Iraq and King Saud of Saudi Arabia. Amidst these recriminations, the Americans introduced the Eisenhower Doctrine which promised massive aid to any nation renouncing all links with the Communist Bloc. Such a move was bound to be seen by Nasser as an American attempt at neo-colonialism calculated to fill the gap left by the retreating British Empire. Turkey, claiming an insecure border with Syria, massed forces accordingly. The United States, in response, misguidedly announced plans to help arm Turkey, Jordan, Iraq and Lebanon. In turn, Nasser airlifted Egyptian troops into Syria. This rapprochement with Syria led to a clamour for union between the two countries when the crisis eventually subsided.

Nasser responded with purely Arab sentiment without any effort to build the economic, political and geographical infrastructures necessary for such a union to succeed. The United Arab Republic (U.A.R.) lasted less than four years. A mixture of Egyptian highhandedness and bureaucratic incompetence led to intense Syrian disaffection. With Amer governing the Syrian province and allowing all-pervasive corruption and nepotism the union was doomed from early on.

The establishment of the U.A.R. sent tremors of panic through neighbouring countries like Lebanon, Jordan, Iraq and Saudi Arabia—not to mention Israel. As Lebanon accepted the Eisenhower Doctrine, the Egyptians increased their attacks on its President. By the spring of 1958 Lebanon was in a virtual state of civil war. As Nasser's agents fomented and aided the Lebanese rebellion, Brigadier Kassem staged a bloody revolution which ended monarchic rule in Iraq. American marines landed in Lebanon and British troops arrived in Amman. The crisis was diffused with the election of a new Lebanese President acceptable to all sides.

During that period Nasser clamped down on Egyptian and Syrian Communists with unparalleled ferocity much to his Soviet allies' chagrin. Relationships with the Russians deteriorated considerably although Russian loans and aid did not cease. With the Iraqi regime moving further into the Communist camp, Nasser backed an attempted rebellion that went disastrously wrong. Eventually the Iraqi and Syrian régimes were replaced by Baathist governments that were more amenable to Nasser's brand of Pan-Arabism. In a meeting that lasted several weeks the three countries tried to reach an agreement over a tripartite union. The verbatim scripts of these meetings show Nasser's method of handling fellow Arab leaders. With an encyclopaedic knowledge of all relevant data, he was able to spring one uncomfortable trap after another on them. Mixed with this was his inherent ability to remember much of the past. There are, in the scripts, endless references to the previous union and to previous meetings. The whole thing reads like a worst kind of family reunion script. Although the meetings ended with a skeletal agreement on unity, nothing came of it.

During the same period Nasser established a regular correspondence with President Kennedy. There was considerable empathy between the two men that may have led to a course of events different from that which occurred after Kennedy's assassination. With the advent of the more truculent Johnson, Nasser knew that he had to deal with an outright supporter of Israel.

In the early sixties, having been thoroughly buffeted by internecine Arab intrigues, Nasser turned his attentions to supporting black African revolutionaries. Again, his principle of Pan-Africanism backfired as Israel, with her superior aid and technology, outpaced him. Nasser felt passionately about third world neutralism. Non-alignment—or positive neutralism—was regarded with intense suspicion by the super powers, especially the Americans. Because of this belief, and because of his conviction in nations' rights to rid themselves of all forms of colonialism, Nasser was constantly being forced into imbroglios which were hard to see through or to come out of.

One such involvement was what he came to refer to as "my Vietnam." General Sallal staged a successful coup in the Yemen against his new Imam who sought refuge in Saudi Arabia. With Royalist forces regrouping, Sallal appealed to Nasser for help. Nasser responded instantly as befitting the symbolic head of the Arab world. This was a decision that he was later to regret bitterly. For the next eight years Egypt was locked in bitter struggles against the Saudi Arabians in the harsh and unfamiliar Yemeni territory. Egypt's strength—both military and economic—was thoroughly sapped by the time Israel launched its destructive forces five years later.

On the home front Nasser was faring no better. In the early sixties he launched a major nationalisation programme that eventually increased the already notorious crippling bureaucracy whilst stifling further industrial progress and productivity. Amidst all this there were two shining stars that maintained, or indeed increased, the Arabs' love for him. The first was the completion of the first stage of the Aswan High Dam. This symbolic technological feat became part of legendary folklore. Like some unaccountable miracle, it hoisted the Arab's perception of herself or himself from being an oriental subject race to a dignified member of the twentieth century technological age—never mind that the Russians made it possible. The second star in Nasser's heaven was the proclamation of the National Charter securing a say for all humble Egyptians in the governance of their country. The Charter also accorded equal rights to women and put family planning firmly on the agenda of an over-populated nation.

In his *Philosophy of the Revolution* Nasser wrote: "within the Arab circle there is a role wandering aimlessly in search of a hero."

Whether Nasser turned out to be that hero, or whether that role would still be held by anybody else, was a question that trembled on every Arab's lips in June 1967. For a short historic and salubrious theatrical period the role was no longer aimless. The hero seemed to fill it to perfection.

The Battle for Palestine

After the rupture of the Egyptian-Syrian union, Nasser went into isolation during which he seemed to undergo a character change. There is little firsthand evidence of his deeper motives for isolating himself. The Syrian secession quite clearly shook him. He felt personally betrayed especially since, contrary to all advice and appearances, he refused to believe such a rupture possible. After all, on his last visit to Damascus, he was mobbed by a massive adoring and hysterical crowd. Nasser, however, had made three mistakes. Firstly, he had assumed that his own overwhelming personal popularity ensured the continuance of the union. Secondly, he did not calculate on the Syrians' levantine entrepreneurial business spirit and acquisitive culture: the Syrians were not a docile people like their Egyptian counterparts. Thirdly, Nasser made the cardinal error of all family patriarchs in assuming that all his children were alike, of one mind, subject to his overwhelming national logic. They were not so.

No wonder, then, that the breakup of the U.A.R. seemed to touch his very soul. Added to all of this, the Pan-Arab in him knew that, without unity, the Arabs were doomed to wander in between obscurantism and a thin veneer of modernism: confused, powerless and spiritually exiled.

During his brief retreat Nasser was irritable and overtly suspicious of colleagues. He seemed to lose his much admired and slightly zany sense of humour. It was during this period that he surrounded himself with yes-men and toadies. His suspicions led him to dismiss many able and intelligent men. Characteristically, however, he retained, and, indeed, promoted, Amer, despite all indications as to the Field Marshal's unsuitability for any post let alone the sensitive First Vice-Presidential one.

Eventually, and possibly as a reaction, Nasser re-emerged to set in motion some drastically innovative domestic measures like increased nationalisation and the National Charter.

Since 1948, the Palestine question had dogged the Arab political scene. Nasser, fully aware that Israel was there to stay, attempted to silence hotheads around him by paying lip service to the Palestinians' right of return. In the Gaza strip, he set in motion an economic and social programme that brought dramatic improvements to the local population. After the 1956 war Nasser relied heavily on the United Nations forces to keep Egypt's borders with Israel clear of incidents.

But the Palestinian question was not going to go away. It was, in fact, going to cause Nasser to become a reactive politician whose proactive skills seemed to disappear since the halcyon days of 1956.

The first of a set of events that caused Nasser to lose the initiative came in the mid-sixties. Relations with the West had become strained. Nasser was seen as an arrogant upstart who needed to be brought down a peg or two. In return Nasser became increasingly suspicious of Western machinations—real or imaginary. A series of misunderstandings, coupled with the Americans' incompetence in handling communications and public relations, caused Nasser to decide that the United States was attempting to control Egypt's foreign policy by using its wheat shipments as a bargaining counter. British behaviour in Aden led him to believe that the Western powers were about to stage another Suez. Coupled with all of this were the runaway events in the Middle East itself.

Nasser found himself unable to extricate his forces from the Yemeni war. With tensions between Israel and Syria rising over Palestinian raids across the border, Nasser's prestige as the Arab supremo stood to suffer if he did not intervene on Syria's behalf. It became a matter of political necessity for Nasser to adopt a militant posture. He lacked the popular support necessary for pragmatic politics. Some might say that he lacked the political leadership required to take proactive decisions which might have been politically unpopular. Nasser, therefore, continued to react to events without a seeming overall plan.

He backed the formation of the Palestine Liberation Organisation (P.L.O.) although he kept it under tight control. The new P.L.O. leader Shukhairy's constant bombastic rhetoric on the destruction of Israel gained the Jewish state overwhelming sympathy in the West. Neither were many Arab régimes averse to having Nasser's pedestal pulled out from underneath him.

Whilst the Arab world floundered in a sea of intrigue and counter-intrigue, Israel built up its economic and military machines into a state of preparedness far superior to her Arab enemies. Ben Gurion, Dayan and other Israeli hawks never lost an opportunity to urge their government to take a more hostile stance to Egypt. Nasser became the archenemy whose removal still remained Ben Gurion's main aim. By 1966, Israel's government, under Eshkol, succumbed to pressure and launched several reprisal attacks against Syria and Jordan. Nasser, with the United Nations forces on his border, did not react.

Such a state of affairs could not remain for long. Nasser's Pan-Arab prestige came under attack from almost every Arab quarter. After Israel's attack on Jordan, Hussein taunted him with cowardice and revisionism. Others wondered aloud as to why Nasser was killing Yemeni Arabs and standing by whilst Israel killed Syrian, Jordanian and Palestinian Arabs.

Under such heavy pressure Nasser signed a mutual defence treaty with Syria, later joined by Jordan. With increased Israeli attacks the tension rose to the point where Nasser asked the U.N. troops to stage a partial withdrawal from Egyptian territory. This act seemed to be a bluff since the United Nations was being asked to make a nominal withdrawal. It backfired. The United Nations withdrew completely leaving Egyptian and Israeli forces face to face. Nasser precipitated the crisis by blockading the Straits of Tiran and closing the Gulf of Akaba to Israeli shipping. He was probably still bluffing with the hope of twisting Israel's arm into some form of backdown. During that period he made constant references to the Suez gamble. Despite overwhelming advice to the contrary from his advisers and ministers, he deployed his forces accordingly. The gamble did not pay off.

On June 5, 1967 Israel launched a massive assault against Egypt, Syria and Jordan. Its better equipped army coupled with its soldiers' superior motivation and the enemy's criminal incompetence and lack of preparedness, Israel inflicted a humiliating defeat on Egypt, Syria and Jordan.

More importantly, Israel smashed through the pretence of Arab unity, irreparably cracked the mirror of Nasser's revolutionary achievements and sent him hurtling into his, and the Arabs', darkest hour from which they never fully emerged.

Declining Years and Death

After the defeat of 1967, Nasser's position in the Arab world was never to be the same again. He rapidly became isolated as he tried to extricate Egypt from her post-defeat despair. Even then, his position as Egypt's only possible leader remained very strong. This was shown by the huge public clamour for his return after his resignation at the end of the war.

Nasser took upon himself the heavy responsibility of the Arabs' defeat. His health deteriorated sharply leading to a minor heart attack followed by several visits to Russia for prolonged treatment.

Amer paid the price for his criminal neglect of Egypt's security by being stripped of all offices. Soon afterwards he was implicated in a plot to overthrow Nasser's government. Even at this late stage, Nasser tried to give Amer a way out first by offering him exile immediately after the war and then by refusing to be drawn into signing a death warrant. In the end Amer committed suicide.

Nasser's first aim was to rebuild Egypt's flagging army. He threw himself at the Soviets' mercy. Within two years Egypt's armed forces were back to their pre-1967 strength although under direct control of Soviet advisers and trainers.

Egypt's second priority was to regain her conquered lands. Nasser was enough of a pragmatist to know that armed force against the superior Israelis would not work. He worked hard to reach a settlement through the United Nations. Egypt accepted U.N. Resolution 242 with its implicit recognition of the state of Israel. It also accepted the United States Rogers Peace Plan and welcomed U.N. mediator Jarring on his shuttle diplomacy. Meanwhile, Nasser kept up the pressure through a costly war of attrition across the Suez Canal.

Ironically, Nasser's pragmatism made him align himself with his erstwhile foes, the Arab reactionary governments of Jordan's Hussein and Faysal of Saudi Arabia. This alienated him from the mainstream Arab nationalists such as Syria, Iraq and the P.L.O. Saudi Arabia and Kuwait agreed to pay Egypt substantial sums in reparation after the Khartoum Arab Summit. Nasser also re-established diplomatic links with London in an attempt to gain access to the Americans whom he believed held the key to an Arab-Israeli settlement. Finally, he withdrew all the Egyptian forces out of Yemen in the next three years.

This late stage pragmatism did not pay off. Israel's government was now led by Golda Meir who, influenced by right wing politicians like Menachim Begin, seemed reluctant to cede anything to the Arabs. After annexing Arab East Jerusalem, Israel proceeded to allow strategically placed Jewish settlements to spring up on the occupied territories. On the other hand, the Americans, ever more suspicious of Russian influence in Egypt, continued their diplomatic and practical support for Israel's position.

After the Rogers Plan succeeded in establishing a cease-fire between Egypt and Israel, Egypt had to face three new problems. Economically, the country was in trouble with the Canal zone virtually destroyed and the Canal itself still blocked. Syria and Iraq increased their verbal attacks on Nasser for what they claimed was his abandonment of the Palestinians. The Palestinians themselves had undergone major traumatic changes as a result of the June war. They were no longer willing to wait for other Arabs to regain their homeland. The P.L.O., under the new leadership of Arafat, started to build up an army with a view to waging war by the Palestinians and for the Palestinians. Along with this small army the P.L.O. was also building a highly successful infrastructure in refugee camps in Jordan and especially in Lebanon. However, Arafat could not entirely control his fractious organisation. Consequently, the Popular Front for the Liberation of Palestine (P.F.L.P.) increased its spectacular publicity seeking attacks on neutral territories abroad. Also by the end of 1969 the P.L.O. itself had stepped up its attacks on Israel thus attracting massive Israeli retaliation on the P.L.O.'s host countries. This new found zest by the P.L.O. was largely the result of a Palestinian-Jordanian victory in the battle for Karameh which severely dented Israel's legend of invincibility.

Nasser made supreme efforts to tone down P.L.O. activities. By then his assumed leadership of the Arab world was largely a thing of the past. He was seen by the Palestinians as a man who cared only for Egypt. They, and only they, cared for Palestine.

After an appeal from Arafat, Nasser managed to secure an agreement separating P.L.O. and Lebanese forces in south Lebanon. He never lived to see the disastrous results of this 1969 agreement. It was but a temporary measure which only postponed the day when, the once peaceful and entrepreneurial Lebanese were to dive headlong into an internecine civil war of unfathomable savagery.

Nasser had more success in his very last act. In September of 1970 Hussein's patience snapped after the P.F.L.P. blew up three hijacked aircraft on Jordanian territory. He launched a massive war to rid his Kingdom of Palestinian guerrillas. An Arab summit was called in Egypt during which Nasser, showing signs of his old dynamism, sense of humour, herculean physical prowess and tightrope diplomacy managed to get King Hussein and Chairman Arafat to sign a peace agreement thus successfully adjourning the conference.

He died that same day.

Nasser's main achievements were to instill a sense of dignity in his people—both Egyptian and Arab. In Egypt he started to educate his people as workers within a modern industrial society. Workers' lives were regulated by standard working hours, health care and pension rights. Land distribution became more equitable under his Presidency. Output was increased four-fold by 1970. The Aswan High Dam allowed Egypt to feed her rapidly increasing population. To a large measure, Egypt's successes after 1973, including its peace settlement with Israel, were due to Nasser's latter day pragmatism.

Although he gave the Arabs that much needed hallmark of independent nationhood, dignity, he failed in his attempts to unite them in any way. It may be said that Nasser was attempting the impossible. If he were a latter-day Saladin, then the odds were heavily stacked against him. He could be best described as a dynamic force whose opportunities were created by forces beyond his control but which opportunities he must take part of the blame for mishandling. At best he was an Arab hero with a tragic flaw, at worst he was out of his political depth.

Perhaps the last word should be left to Malraux who said, "Regardless of everything, regardless of success or failure, victory or defeat, Nasser will go down in history as the embodiment of Egypt, just as Napoleon became the embodiment of France." To many Arabs Nasser was the everlasting embodiment of their very being.

Chronology of the Life of Gamal Abdel Nasser

1918	January	Nasser born in Alexandria, Egypt
1936		wounded by a bullet during an anti-British mass protest organised by himself as President of the Secondary Students' Association
1937	March	accepted as an officer cadet at the Military Academy, starts to study English
1938		receives his first posting as an infantry subaltern at Mankabad
1939		volunteers for service in the Sudan along with Abdel Hakim Amer, outbreak of World War II
1942	January	King Farouk capitulates to British military threat and appoints a Wafdist Government led by Nahas
	September	promoted to Captain
1943	February	appointed instructor at the Military Academy, makes contacts to form the incipient Free Officers' movement
1944		protocol agreeing to form Arab League signed, Nasser meets Tahia whom he marries a year later, Jewish revolt led by the Haganah and Stern groups starts in Palestine
1945	March	Arab League formally established
1946		Bevin-Sidky Protocol agrees to the withdrawal of all British forces from Egypt by 1949

1947	November	United Nations General Assembly agrees to partition Palestine into separate Palestinian Arab and Jewish states
1948	April	250 Palestinians at Deir Yassin massacred by Jewish extremists
	May	Britain leaves Palestine, Israel declares its independence, Egypt, Iraq, Syria, Lebanon and Transjordan invade Palestine
	July	wounded in the battle for Negba
	October	second truce of the war broken, Nasser's troops surrounded at Falluja, fierce counterattack led by him
1949	February	armistice signed by warring sides, Nasser returns to Egypt as campaign hero, Palestinian Gaza strip under Egyptian control
	October	Free Officers agree to launch their revolution in five years
1950		newly elected Wafd government brings some relief from repression allowing the Free Officers to publicise their cause, Nasser elected President of the Free Officers' Executive Committee
1951	October	1936 Treaty and 1899 Condominium agreement abrogated by the Egyptians
	December	British forces attack and destroy a village
1952	January	Ismailia police post attacked by the British, Cairo riots, Free Officers nominate General Neguib as President of the Officers' Club in opposition to King Farouk's nominee, Free Officers' six point manifesto agreed upon
	June	General Neguib elected President of the Free Officers' Executive with Nasser as Vice-President and Chief of Staff
	July	Free Officers under threat of arrest, July 23rd bloodless coup successfully carried out, Revolutionary Command Council (R.C.C.) formed, King Farouk abdicates and leaves Egypt
	October	Kermit Roosevelt visits Cairo, William Foster, United States Assistant Secretary for Defence, recommends

		U.S. arms sale to Egypt (later vetoed by Britain)
1953	January	R.C.C. takes over the government from the Wafd
	February	Anglo-Egyptian agreement on equity of surveillance of the Sudan signed
	June	Egypt proclaimed a republic with Neguib as President and Prime Minister, Nasser made Deputy Prime Minister
1954		Nasser starts secret contacts with Israeli Premier Moshe Sharett lasting until February 1955, after an internal power struggle Nasser becomes Prime Minister and later assumes the functions of the Presidency
	July	France agrees to supply Israel with jet fighters
	October	Anglo-Egyptian agreement on total British withdrawal and joint operation of the Suez Canal signed, the 1888 Constantinople Convention on freedom of navigation through Suez is upheld, failed assassination attempt against Nasser leads to the suppression of the Moslem Brotherhood
1955	February	despite ceaseless efforts by Nasser to prevent it the Baghdad Pact is signed by Britain, Pakistan and Iran later in the year, Eden visits Cairo, Israel raids Gaza, Nasser agrees to allow fedayeen volunteers to strike into Israel, first meeting with Tito of Yugoslavia
	March	Egypt, Syria and Saudi Arabia sign defence agreement
	April	Russia accepts Egypt's request for arms supplies, Nasser's approaches to Britain and the United States rejected, first commercial agreement with Russia concluded, Afro-Asian conference held at Bandung in Indonesia
	July	Russo-Egyptian arms deal concluded after Washington refuses a last minute appeal from Nasser
	December	U.S. sponsored Anderson peace mission fails
1956		Under Ben Gurion, Israel intensifies attacks on the Gaza strip
	February	King Hussein of Jordan dismisses General Glubb as Commander of the Arab Legion, Egypt's relations

		with Britain deteriorate, World Bank loan agreement to build the Aswan High Dam announced
	May	Western powers agree on sale of arms to Israel, Egypt buys MIGs from Russia, Egypt recognizes Communist China
	July	France captures Algerian leader, the U.S. and Britain renege on their promised loan for the Aswan High Dam, Nasser nationalises the Suez Canal
	September	Canal users' proposals on Suez rejected by Egypt, Suez Canal Company increases its efforts to scuttle Egypt's attempts to keep the Canal going, Dulles' Suez Canal Users' Association scheme collapses, France secretly pledges support for a one year old Dayan plan for invading Gaza and Sinai, Britain invited to join the scheme
	October	Israel invades Egypt, Britain and France issue pre-arranged ultimatum to Israel and Egypt which is rejected by the latter, tripartite attack against Egypt begins
	December	British withdraw from Egypt, Israel follows suit in March 1957 after which the Suez Canal is reopened, Nasser diagnosed diabetic
1957	March	Jordan ends 1948 treaty with Britain
	August	troops massed on Turco-Syrian border, Egyptian troops despatched to Syria
1958	January	Iraq and Jordan form the Arab Union, Lebanon accepts American aid under the Eisenhower Doctrine
	February	Egypt and Syria become the United Arab Republic (U.A.R.)
	May	goaded by the U.A.R., Lebanon's Moslems rebel against the Christian President
	July	Iraqi Royal Family killed and republic declared, U.S. marines land in Lebanon, British forces arrive in Jordan
	October	relations between the U.A.R. and Tunisia broken
	December	purge against Communists starts in the U.A.R.

1959	March	U.A.R. backed Mosul rebellion crushed in Iraq
	October	Field Marshal Amer appointed viceroy in Syria
	November	final Russo-Egyptian agreement on the Aswan High Dam signed
	December	diplomatic relations with Britain restored
1960	May	Egyptian press nationalised
	July	Iran recognizes Israel, U.A.R. breaks diplomatic relations with Iran
	September	Nasser visits the United States for the U.N. General Assembly session, he meets Eisenhower, MacMillan, Krushchev and other world leaders
1961	February	Egyptian arms shipments sent to Congolese rebels
	June	confrontation with Iraq over Kuwait, British troops in Kuwait
	September	the U.A.R. breaks up after a coup in Syria, Nasser withdraws into isolation suffering from nervous tension, his health deteriorates considerably, first Non-aligned conference held in Belgrade, U.S.S.R. resumes nuclear testing
	October	Egypt embarks on major nationalisation programme, diplomatic relations with Jordan ruptured
1962	May	National Charter proclaimed
	July	Algeria declared independent
	September	General Abdullah Sallal stages a Nasserist coup-d'état in the Yemen
	October	Egyptian troops sent to bolster Sallal's régime in the Yemen against the Imam's Saudi backed forces, Sino-Indian border war
1963	February	Iraqi coup-d'état places pro-Nasser Baathist group in power
	March	Syrian coup-d'état brings Baath to power, Egyptian-Syrian-Iraqi tripartite union abortive talks start
	April	the short-lived federated union between Egypt, Syria and Iraq announced

	August	Israel starts work to divert the Jordan River
	October	Algerian-Moroccan hostilities over the Sahara end with compromise settlement after Nasser's shipment of arms to Algeria
	November	Kennedy assassinated, Johnson becomes President
1964	January	resumption of Egyptian-Jordanian diplomatic relations, major Arab summit conference held
	March	Amer becomes Nasser's First Vice-President thus heir apparent
	May	the first stage of the Aswan High Dam completed, Krushchev attends inauguration just before he is ousted in a Kremlin Palace coup, Palestine Liberation Organisation (P.L.O.) launched by the Palestine Congress
	July	second Non-aligned conference held in Cairo
	September	P.L.O. sanctioned by Arab Summit
1965	March	Tunisian President Bourguiba calls for peace with Israel, Egyptian diplomatic relations with Tunisia severed
	April	Egyptian diplomatic relations broken off with West Germany
	June	Boumedienne seizes power in Algeria
	September	Moslem Brotherhood members lead violent demonstrations in Cairo, Arab Socialist Union (A.S.U.) formed to educate Egyptians in Nasser's brand of socialism
1966	February	Atassi assumes Presidency of Syria after successful coup-d'état, Iraq under new President, Jordan withdraws its ambassador from Egypt
	September	Israel launches retaliatory attack against Syria
	November	Egypt and Syria sign mutual defence pact, massive Israeli strike into Jordan
1967	April	Israel mounts air attack against Syria
	May	state of alert declared in Egypt, United Nations forces told to leave Egyptian territory, Egypt blockades

		Gulf of Akaba, Egyptian forces move into Sharm el-Sheikh, Dayan appointed Israel's Minister of Defence as hawks take over the cabinet, Hussein joins Egyptian-Syrian defence alliance
	June	American peace proposals accepted by Egypt, Israel attacks Egypt, Syria and Jordan occupying the West Bank of the Jordan River (Eastern Palestine), Gaza, Sinai and the Golan Heights, Egypt breaks off diplomatic relations with the United States, Nasser resigns and is reinstated after massive national clamour, Amer dismissed from army command and vice-presidency, President Nasser takes on the Premiership and the army command
	July	Khartoum Arab Summit decides to compensate Egypt and Jordan for their war losses, Syria boycotts the Summit, Egypt committed to withdrawal from the Yemen
	September	Amer arrested, he commits suicide
	November	United Nations Resolution 242 adopted and accepted by Egypt, diplomatic relations with Britain reinstated, Aden declared independent by the British
1968	January	United States agrees to supply Israel with jet aircraft after Eshkol's visit to Johnson
	March	P.L.O. victory at Karameh
	July	Nasser admitted to Russian sanatorium as his health deteriorates, new Iraqi régime joins Syria in stepping up anti-Nasser attacks
1969	February	Golda Meir becomes Israeli Prime Minister
	September	U.S. Phantom jets delivered to Israel
	November	Nasser hits out at the Americans as the Suez Canal war of attrition intensifies, Nasser succeeds in getting the P.L.O. and Lebanon to sign an agreement limiting Palestinian activities on Lebanese soil
	December	Nasser successfully requests Russian SAM ground-to-air missiles manned by Soviet troops, Rabat Arab Summit isolates Nasser
1970	May	Yemeni war is over

June   Americans announce the Rogers Plan to achieve a temporary cease fire between Egypt and Israel

July   Egypt accepts the Rogers Peace Plan, P.L.O. radio stations closed in Egypt

September   four airliners are hijacked by the Popular Front for the Liberation of Palestine (P.F.L.P.), Hussein declares martial law as intense fighting errupts between the P.L.O. and Jordanian Royal forces, Nasser succeeds in achieving a peaceful settlement in Jordan, he dies of a heart attack

October   Nasser buried

I. Manuscripts, Newspapers, Periodicals and Archival Sources

Dar el Kutub, Kornish el Nil in Cairo, is the Egyptian National Archive Centre where material on and by Nasser may be found. The Centre houses books, newspapers and magazines in Arabic. Researchers able to read Arabic will find here an exhaustive supply of Nasser's speeches, statements and related Egyptian archival sources. There are also many English translations.

The University of Durham's Centre for Middle Eastern and Islamic Studies contains one of the world's most comprehensive collection of primary documents concerning the Middle East. Enquiries to: University Microfilms Ltd., St. John's Road, Tylers Green, High Wycombe, Bucks HP10 8HR, United Kingdom. Telephone: Penn (049 481) 3844.

The *BBC Summary of World Broadcasts*, part 4, Middle East, is available from the BBC Monitoring Service, Reading, Berkshire BG4 8TZ. Telephone: Reading (0734) 472742.

A. U.S. Government Sources

1. *Congressional Quarterly Almanac 1952–1970*. Washington, D.C.: Congressional Quarterly Service.

A brief but useful reference source on the United States' political responses to major Middle East events. Entries under Nasser, Gamal Abdel, Middle-East and Egypt or United Arab Republic.

2. *Council on Foreign Relations*. Documents on American Foreign Relations, New York: Simon and Schuster, annual.

3. *Facts on File Five-Year Index* started in 1946. Index Editor: Dorothy Kattleman. New York, FACTS ON FILE INC.

A useful quick reference guide to events.

4. *Public Papers of the Presidents of the United States*: Containing the Public Messages, Speeches, and Statements of the President. Published annually by the Office of the Federal Register. Washington, D.C.: U.S. Government Printing Office.

The Presidents under whose name each volume(s) appears during Nasser's time are: Eisenhower, Kennedy, Johnson and Nixon.

5. United States Department of State. American Foreign Policy Current Documents begun in 1950 as follows: *A Decade of American Foreign Policy: Basic Documents, 1941-1949*. Senate Document 123, 81st Congress, 1st Session. Washington, D.C. : U.S. Government Printing Office, 1950.

6. *American Foreign Policy, 1950–1955: Basic Documents*. Department of State Publication 6446. Washington, D.C.: U.S. Government Printing Office, 1957.

7. *American Foreign Policy: Current Documents*, annually for 1956–1967.

8. United States Department of State. *The Department of State Bulletin, 1952–1970*. Washington, D.C.: U.S. Government Printing Office, 1952–1970.

9. United States Department of State. *Foreign Relations of the United States*, volume IX: *The Near and Middle East*;

10. volume XIV: *Arab-Israeli Dispute 1955*;

11. volume XV: *Arab-Israeli Dispute January 1–July 26, 1956;*

12. and most recently published, volume XXVI: *Suez Canal Crisis, July 27–December 31, 1956*. Washington, D.C.: U.S. Government Printing Office, 1986–1989.

Gives all the documentary material relevant to major foreign policy decisions of the U.S.

13. U.S. Department of State. *The Suez Canal Problem: July 26–September 22, 1956: A Documentary Publication*. Washington, D.C.: U.S. Government Publishing Office, 1956.

Including texts of agreements and treaties on the legal status of the Canal.

14. U.S. Department of State. *United States Policy in the Middle East: September 1956–June 1957, Documents.* Washington, D.C.: Government Printing Office, 1957.

Includes documents on: U.S. Middle East policy, reactions to developments and related issues.

15. U.S. Senate. Committee on Foreign Relations. *Executive Sessions of the Senate Foreign Relations Committee.* 84th Congress, 2nd Session, 1956. Historical Series, volume 8. Washington, D.C.: Government Printing Office, 1978.

Secret hearings covering debate over the Aswan Dam, mutual security programmes for the Middle East and the Mutual Security Act of 1956. Made public in 1978.

16. U.S. Senate. Committee on Foreign Relations. Hearings on the Eisenhower Doctrine. *Executive Session of the Senate Foreign* Relations Committee, together with Joint Session with the Senate Armed Services Committee. 85th Congress, 1st Session, 1957. Historical Series, volume 9. Washington, D.C.: Government Printing Office, 1979.

Released to the public in December 1979.

See also: Chapter VI, section A.

B. U.K. Government Sources

There is an index of Foreign Office papers at Kew (Class List). There exists also a published index: Public Record Office, London. *Lists and Indeces, Supplementary Series, List of Foreign Office Records*, volumes 15, 27 and part II (for 1951). None of these indices covers the Nasser period. Nonetheless, there are papers cited relevant to Egypt during Nasser's youth. A knowledge of Egypt's history during the first half of the twentieth century is essential for an understanding of Nasser's political career. Kraus-Thomson Organization Limited, Millwood, New York, 1974.

17. Cabinet Office (CAB): *CAB 128* and *129*, 1949–1959.

Cabinet Office papers relating to Egypt and Nasser.

18. *CAB* 130. AD-HOC Committees General and Miscellaneous Series.

19. Colonial Office (CO): *CO 537 Palestine Files.*

20. *CO 733 Palestine Correspondence.*

21. Foreign Office (FO): *FO 406.* Confidential Print. Egypt and the Sudan 1839–1958. Pieces 226 to 237 (1947–1958) have been closed for fifty years.

22. *FO 24.* Pieces 1–6. General Correspondence 1785–1818.

23. *FO 141.* Embassy and Consular Archives 1825–1952.

24. *FO 841.* Embassy and Consular Archives 1830–1949.

25. *FO 846* and *847.* Embassy and Consular Archives 1858–1947.

26. *FO 891.* Embassy and Consular Archives 1911-1956. 1955 has been closed for fifty years.

27. *FO 926.* Embassy and Consular Archives 1827–1948.

28. *FO 371.* General Political Correspondence Egypt. 1952–1959 are currently available. Background information on Egypt may be consulted from 1906 onwards.

29. *FO 848.* The Milner Mission.

In 1919 Britain announced its intention to preserve Egypt's autonomy under British protection. Lord Milner's mission was to work out a policy for Egyptian self-government.

30. *FO 921.* Minister of State, Cairo. 1942–1946. Piece 306 on Syria and Lebanon has been closed for fifty years.

See also: Chapter VI, section A.

C. Periodicals and Newspapers

All periodicals and newspapers with articles specifically on Nasser are listed. Also listed are newspapers that gave regular extensive coverage on Nasser during his lifetime. These are given as a general reference when they are likely to be less known to Western readers. Such references are given only once in order to direct readers to less obvious sources of regular information. The Chronology of the Life of Gamal Abdel Nasser may be used as a guide in researching into such newspapers. More specific dates may be extracted from the sections on *The London Times* and *The New York Times* (See chapter I, section D). Obvious Western periodicals are only mentioned where an article has been cited.

31. *Al-Ahram* (The Pyramids). An Egyptian daily.

32. *Al-Akhbar* (The News). An Egyptian daily.

33. *The Arab Chronicle*. London.

34. *The Arab Observer*. Cairo.

35. *Arab Report and Record*. London.

36. *The Arab World*. Beirut: since 1969.

37. *Asian Affairs*. "Nasser and after: a Symposium." February 1971: 12+.

38. *Business Week*. "Egypt Turns Friendlier to West." November 28th 1959: 107+.

39. *Business Week*. "Nasser's Dream Comes a Cropper; Resistance from Socialist Resurrection Party." August 31st 1963: 46+.

40. *Les Cahiers de l'Orient Contemporain* (Notebooks of the Contemporary Orient). Paris. Published quarterly.

41. *Chronology of Arab Politics*. Beirut: 1963.

42. *Commentary*. "Nasser's Decade." Sherman, Alfred. Volume 36, August 1963: 151+.

43. *Daily Star*. A Beirut daily.

44. *Economist*. "The Man with a Past." September 7th 1968: 228+.

45. *Economist*. "The Lost Leader." October 3rd 1970: 13+.

46. *Economist*. "Nasser without His Albatross." January 3rd 1970: 320+.

47. *Economist*. "Nasser Changes Windmills." 28th October 1961: 320+.

48. *Economic Bulletin*. Cairo: National Bank of Egypt, Research Department. 1947—quarterly.

A regular source of information on economic developments and conditions in Egypt including notes, comments and leading articles. Available in Arabic and English.

49. *Economic Indicators*. Cairo: Central Agency for Mobilisations and Statistics, 1952—monthly.

50. *Economic Review*. Cairo: Central Bank of Egypt, 1960—quarterly.

Available in Arabic and English.

51. *L'Égypte Contemporaine* (Contemporary Egypt). Cairo: Society of Political Economy, Statistics and Legislation, 1910—quarterly.

Covers social, economic, political and cultural affairs. Articles in Arabic, English and French.

52. *The Egyptian Gazette*. Cairo.

53. *Al Fatan*. Beirut.

54. *Guardian*. "Ten Years after Suez." July 18th 1966: 8+.

An interview with Nasser.

55. *Guardian*. "President Nasser's Outlook on the Arab World." July 19th 1966: 8+.

56. *Guardian*. "President Nasser Lets down the Arab Revolutionaries." Hirst, David. January 1st 1966: 9+.

57. *Guardian*. "Nasser's Dependence on the Mob." Wall, Michael. June 16th 1967: 11+.

58. *Al-Gumhouriyah* (The Republic). An Egyptian daily.

59. *Institute of Middle East Studies* (Great Britain). "Drama as a Vehicle of Protest in Nasir's Egypt." Semaan, Khalil I. 10 (1), 1979: 49–53.

Analysis of a play by Salah Abd al-Sabur that is extremely critical of Nasser's miscalculations.

60. *International and Comparative Law Quarterly*. The Suez Canal, 1969.

Documents relating to the status of the Suez Canal Company from 1854 to 1956.

61. *The Israel Weekly Digest.* Jerusalem.

62. *Jewish Observer and Middle East Review.* London.

63. *Journal of Palestine Studies.* Washington. A quarterly on Palestinian affairs and the Arab-Israeli conflict published jointly by the Institute for Palestine Studies and Kuwait University.

64. *Lissan al-Hal.* Beirut daily.

65. *Life Magazine.* "Nasser and the West." Volume 47, August 10th 1959: 38+.

66. *Life Magazine.* "Nasser's Three Faces to the World." Volume 47, July 20th 1959: 98+.

67. *List of Current Periodicals.* National Library Cataloguing Department. Cairo: National Library Press, 1959. 86 pages.

68. *Majallat al-Iqtisad wa al-Siyasah wa al-Tijarah* (Review of Economics, Politics and Trade). Cairo: Cairo University Press, 1953+.

Each issue contains one article in French or English.

69. *Al-Majallah al-Misriyah lil-Ulum al-Siyasiyah* (Egyptian Political Science Review). Cairo: Egyptian Society of Political Science, 1963+—monthly.

Each issue contains one article in French or English.

70. *Middle Eastern Affairs.* New York: Council for Middle Eastern Affairs, 1950+—monthly.

Current Middle Eastern affairs including Egypt.

71. *Middle Eastern Affairs.* "Egyptian-Syrian Defence Pact." Volume 6, number 11, November 1955: 347–8.

Reproduces the thirteen-article Egyptian-Syrian defence pact which is regarded as an important stage leading to the eventual union between the two countries.

72. *Middle Eastern Affairs.* "Syrian Break from the United Arab Republic." Volume 12, number 9, November 1961: 269–78.

Reprints the statement made by Nasser after Syria's secession from the United Arab Republic.

73. *Middle East Economist.* "Suez Canal Achievements since 1956." July-August 1962: 246–247.

74. *The Middle East Forum.* Beirut.

75. *Middle East Journal.* "The Egyptian-Israeli Peace Treaty." Volume 33, number 3, Summer 1979: 327–46.

Although an event that took place after his death, Nasser had done much to lay the ground for an eventual resolution of the problem.

76. *Middle East News Economic Weekly.* Cairo: Middle East News Agency, 1962+ —weekly.

Reports also include other Arab countries as well as Egypt.

77. *Middle East Observer.* Cairo: 8 Chawarby Street. An English language weekly.

An English language weekly.

78. *Middle Eastern Studies.* London: Cass, 1964+—quarterly.

Despite a strong historical bias also includes articles on contemporary affairs.

79. *Mideast Mirror.* Beirut. Published weekly.

80. *Nahar.* Beirut daily.

81. *National Review.* "Colonel Sends His Compliments." Volume 17, January 12th 1965: 10+.

82. *The New Middle East.* London.

83. *New Outlook.* Tel Aviv.

84. *New Republic.* "Two on an Arab Summit." Magruder, Calvert. Volume 140, June 29th 1959: 6+.

85. *New Republic.* "Middleman in Mid-career." Monroe, Elizabeth. Volume 143, November 28th 1960: 24+.

86. *New Statesman.* "Nasser's Comeback." March 15th 1963: 366+.

87. *New Statesman.* "Conversation with Nasser." Kingsley, Martin. January 5th 1962: 6+.

88. *Newsweek Magazine.* "Nervous Nasser." Volume 71, March 18th 1968: 65+.

89. *Newsweek Magazine.* "Feet of Clay." Volume 72, December 9th 1968: 46+.

On student demonstrations against Nasser.

90. *Newsweek Magazine.* "Rumblings out of Cairo." Volume 74, September 29th 1969: 49+.

91. *Newsweek Magazine.* "No Other Way for Us but Force." Volume 74, November 17th 1969: 61+.

On Arab-Jewish relations.

92. *New York Times Magazine.* "Nasserism Stirs up the Middle East." May 19th 1963: 10+.

93. *New York Times Magazine.* "Nasser's Drives: Inside Egypt and Beyond." January 10th 1960: 12+.

94. *Orient.* Paris. Published quarterly until 1968.

95. *L'Orient.* Beirut daily. Now incorporated with *Le Jour.*

96. *Record of the Arab World.* Beirut. Published monthly.

97. *Saturday Review.* "Portrait of a Sensitive Plotter." Schmidt, Dana Adams. Volume 42, April 25th 1959: 17+.

98. *Saturday Review.* "Portrait of a Self-made Pharoah." Stringer, William H. Volume 43, December 3rd 1960: 26+.

99. *The Scribe.* Cairo.

100. *Senior Scholastic.* "Shifting Sands of Arab Union." Volume 83, January 17th 1964: 8+.

101. *Time Magazine.* "Egypt: the Two New Faces of Nasser." Volume 107, January 12th 1976: 24+.

Nasser is venerated as a prophet although not in Egypt.

102. *Time Magazine.* "Nasser Goes Acourtin'." Volume 95, January 12th 1970: 16+.

103. *Time Magazine.* "Nasser's Risky Role in the Middle East." Volume 93, May 16th 1969: 29+.

104. *Time Magazine.* "Change, Change, Change!" Volume 91, March 15th 1968: 28+.

On Nasser's Cairo riots.

105. *Time Magazine.* "Camel Driver." Volume 81, March 29th 1963: 22+.

106. *U.S. News and World Report.* "Why Nasser Acts the Way He Does." Volume 58, January 4th 1965: 30+.

See also:

The London Times. (nos. 107–220).

The New York Times. (nos. 221–308).

Shafik, Fouad Fahmy. *The Press and Politics of Modern Egypt: 1798–1970. A Comparative Analysis of Causal Relationships. (no. 362).*

Shalabieh, Mahmoud Ibrahim. *A Comparison of Political Persuasion on Radio Cairo in the Eras of Nasser and Sadat.* (no. 807).

D. The London Times and The New York Times

There is a great deal on Nasser in the world press of the period. A small selection from *The London Times* and *The New York Times* newspapers is offered here. Where possible references are to similar material from both papers. A great deal may be learnt about Nasser from reading such articles. More significantly, a deeper understanding of Anglo-American attitudes towards him could be achieved through comparing the different stance adopted by each newspaper. Coupled with the section on the Chronology of the Life of Gamal Abdel Nasser, the following entries also provide a panoramic view of Nasser's life, his reactions to events and his eventual enswathement in Western misunderstandings coupled with unmanageable events.

Subjects mentioned are those relating to Nasser in terms of events, statements, foreign responses thereto or his views thereon.

The London Times

1952

107. Egyptian Constitution. December 11th: 7.

108. British Forces in the Canal Zone. December 30th: 4.

1953

109. British Forces in the Canal Zone. January 1st: 8. February 23rd: 5.

110. Relations with Britain. April 6th: 6.

111. British Forces. July 16th: 5. August 13th: 4. August 14th: 8.

112. Anglo-Egyptian Discussions. August 26th: 5.

113. Nasser's Career. February 26th: 2 and 8.

1954

114. Foreign Relations. June 8th: 9.

1955

115. Relations with Israel. March 4th: 8.

116. Nasser. May 4th: 13.

117. Big Power Discussions. July 13th: 6.

118. British Proposals. November 29th: 8.

119. Communism. October 1st: 6.

120. Israel. October 3rd: 3, 4 and 8. October 4th: 6. December 16th: 7.

121. Zionist Organizations in the United States. October 17th: 6th.

1956

122. Iraq. January 28th: 6.

123. Israel. February 20th: 8.

124. The Baghdad Pact. March 26th: 10.

125. Evacuation of British Forces. June 19th: 5 and 10.

126. Foreign Policy. June 2nd: 6. June 20th: 9.

127. Relations with Great Britain. June 18th: 10. June 20th: 9.

128. Nationalization of Suez Canal. July 27th: 2, 4 and 10.

129. Interview with Nasser. September 3rd: 6.

130. Text of the Nationalization of the Suez Canal. September 12th: 6, 7, 8 and 17.

1957

131. Interview with Nasser. January 18th: 6.

132. Anglo-French Intervention. January 18th: 18.

133. Israeli Forces in Egypt. January 18th: 8. February 16th: 6.

134. United States Policy in the Middle East. January 18th: 6. February 2nd: 4. September 10th: 8.

135. Interview with Nasser. March 14th: 8. April 1st: 10. November 16th: 5.

136. Arab Unity. March 14th: 14.

137. Foreign Policy. April 1st: 10.

138. Israel. March 14th: 8.

139. Propaganda. December 7th: 4 and 5.

1958

140. United Arab Republic. February 3rd: 5, 6 and 8. February 24th: 4 and 8.

141. Arab Unity. March 17th: 5 and 8.

142. Iraq-Jordan Federation. March 21st: 5 and 7.

143. Lebanon. May 17th: 5. June 23rd: 7.

144. United Nations Middle East Policy. September 26th: 10.

1959

145. Russia. March 23rd: 9. March 31st: 7. April 18th: 5.

146. Interview with Nasser. April 18th: 5. July 15th: 6.

147. Communism. July 15th: 6.

148. Israel. July 1st: 12. July 27th: 6. July 29th: 7.

149. Relations with Britain, Russia and the United States. December 24th: 6.

1960

150. Israel's Use of the Suez Canal. February 18th: 12. April 26th: 10.

151. Disarmament. April 1st: 4 and 9.

152. Jordanian Leaders. March 8th: 10.

153. Palestinian Refugees. November 8th: 5 and 12.

154. Israel's Nuclear Programme. December 24th: 5.

   1961

155. International Relations. April 24th; 13.

156. Interview with Nasser. May 15th: 14.

157. Labour. July 24th: 8.

158. Arab Unity. October 6th: 14.

159. Economic Situation in Egypt. October 17th: 11.

160. International Relations. September 2nd: 6.

161. Break up of the United Arab Republic. September 30th: 8. October 3rd: 11.

162. Nasser's Policies Reappraised. November 10th: 12.

163. Nationalization of Foreign-owned Land. December 27th: 7.

   1962

164. Foreign Policy. May 22nd: 9.

165. National Charter. May 28th: 11.

166. Free Education. July 28th: 6.

167. Underdeveloped Countries. July 10th: 8.

168. Nasser-Kennedy Correspondence. September 25th: 9.

   1963

169. Troops in the Yemen. January 10th: 9.

170. Creation of Arab Federation. March 17th: 10.

171. German Scientists Working in Egypt. April 2nd: 12.

172. Nasser-Tito Statement. May 18th: 5 and 7.

173. Arab Unity. May 6th: 12.

174. Britain in Yemen. July 2nd: 10.

175. Relations with Israel. July 2nd: 7.

176. Vietnamese Buddhists. October 15th: 10.

177. British Bases in Cyprus. February 24th: 8.

178. British Bases in Libya. February 24th: 8.

   1964

179. Egyptian Forces in Yemen. February 24th: 8.

180. Biographical Note on Field-Marshal Amer. March 25th: 11.

181. South Africa. August 18th: 8.

182. United States Civil Rights Bill. August 18th: 8.

183. International Relations. October 6th: 9.

184. Khrushchev on Nasser. September 16th: 12.

185. Congo. December 24th: 8.

186. Iran. December 24th: 8.

187. United States. December 24th: 8.

   1965

188. The Two Germanies. February 26th: 9.

189. Russia. February 19th: 12.

190. Communism. March 9th: 10.

191. Israel. June 1st: 10.

192. Rhodesia. November 19th: 12.

   1966

193. Iraq's Kurdish Minority. February 21st: 5 and 8.

194. Israel's Nuclear Capability. April 18th: 10.

195. Central Intelligence Agency. August 8th: 6.

196. Joint Statement by Nasser, Tito and Nehru. October 25th: 10.

   1967

197. Arab Summits. February 6th: 8.

198. Rhodesia. April 5th: 5.

199. Arab-Israeli Conflict. May 23rd: 1.

200. Settlement of Arab Israeli War. June 19th: 1.

201. British Policy. May 27th: 1.

202. United States policy. May 4th: 6.

203. Arab-Israeli War. July 24th: 1.

204. Suez Canal. July 20th: 4.

1968

205. Settlement of Arab-Israeli War. February 16th: 7.

206. Interview with Nasser. March 5th: 4.

207. Arab-Israeli Dispute. April 1st: 4.

208. Palestinian Commando Raids. April 19th: 7.

209. Settlement with Israel. April 26th: 6.

210. Nasser's Call for Restraint by Arabs. July 26th: 5.

211. Arab-Israeli Conflict. July 6th: 4.

212. Middle East Settlement. July 24th: 5.

213. Arab-Israeli Dispute. November 8th: 6 and 7.

1969

214. Interview with Nasser. March 5th: 10.

215. Nasser. September 19th: 10.

1970

216. Interview with Nasser. February 19th: 10. May 21st: 6.

217. End of Arab-Israeli Conflict. March 26th: 6.

218. Accepting Political Solution to Arab-Israeli Conflict. July 18th: 4.

219. Obituary of Nasser. September 30th: 12.

220. Arab World after Nasser. November 19th: 6.

See also:

Mikdadi, F. H. "Nasser's Political Humour." August 1st, 1980: 13.

The New York Times

During 1956 and 1967 major entries are also made under "Middle East War."

  1953

221. Threat of Suez Guerrilla Warfare by Nasser. January 3rd: 3.

222. Britain's Terms for Leaving Suez. February 27th: 4. February 28th: 16.

223. Interview with Nasser. April 13th: 6.

224. Egypt's Neutralist Role in Cold War. December 28th: 3.

  1954

225. Nahas's Wife: Corruption and Abuse. March 8th: 3.

226. Anglo-Egyptian Agreement on Suez. July 28th: 1. Text of Agreement. July 28th.

227. Nasser as Revolutionist. September 19th: 12.

  1955

228. United States Arms Sale Offer to Egypt. September 26th: 1.

229. Egypt-U.S.S.R. Cotton for Arms Deal. September 28th: 1.

  1956

230. New Constitution. January 17th: 10.

231. Mrs. Roosevelt's Statement Regarding Arms Sales to Israel. January 29th: 1. Text of Statement. January 29th: 4.

232. United States Withdraws Offer on Aswan High Dam. July 21st: 1.

233. Nasser's Career since 1952. August 5th: 8. August 19th: 7.

234. Suez Canal Nationalized. July 27th: 1.

235. Israel Invades Egypt. October 30th: 1.

236. Anglo-French Ultimatum. October 31st: 1.

237. Nasser on Egyptian Independence. November 22nd: 21.

238. Nasser on all Forms of 'isms.' November 23rd: 26.

1957

239. Egyptianization. January 16th: 1.

240. United States Department Concerned over Russian Arms Sales to Egypt. February 8th: 3.

1958

241. United Arab Republic Proclaimed. February 2nd: 1.

242. Nasser Outlines Arab Unification Programme. February 6th: 1.

243. United Arab States Created. March 9th: 1.

244. Nasser's Policies. March 26th; 36.

245. Nasser on Neutrality Policy. April 23rd: 16.

246. Nasser and Nasserism. July 27th: Section VI, 5.

247. Nasser's Pan-Arabism. August 24th: Section VI, 10.

248. Nasser after Six Years in Power. September 14th: Section IV, 6.

249. Egyptian Media Attack on the United States. October 8th: 1.

1959

250. Nasser's Rift with the West. January 18th: Section IV, 4.

251. Changes in Nasser's Egypt over Ten Years. October 24th: 21.

1960

252. National Union. January 1st: 5.

253. Life in an Egyptian Village. June 4th: 4.

254. Nasser in New York. September 25th: 1 and 36. September 26th: 1 and 16. September 27th: 1 and 19.

255. Israel's List of 23 Alleged Nazis Working in the United Arab Republic. September 30th: 2.

256. Nasser's Bid for Leadership of Neutralist World. December 18th: Section IV, 6.

1961

257. Nasser's Non-Alignment. March 29th: 32.

258. Nasser's Anti-Communism. April 1st: 16.

259. Syrian Withdrawal from the United Arab Republic. October 6th: 3.

260. Break up of the United Arab States. December 27th: 1.

   1962

261. Arms Deal with Russia. January 3rd: 32.

262. Economic Review. January 9th: 65.

263. Nasser's Socialism. March 11th: 2.

264. Nasser's Influence on Arab Socialism. April 8th: Section IV, 4.

265. Survey of Nasser's Arab Socialism. May 25th: 1.

266. National Charter. May 22nd: 1.

267. Nasser's Programme. May 23rd: 44.

   1963

268. German Scientists in Egypt. April 5th: 1. June 10th: 30.

269. Eleven Years of Nasser. July 23rd: 7.

270. Conflict between Egyptianization and Cosmopolitanism. August 31st: 4.

271. United Arab Republic as Symbol of Aspiring ex-Colonial Nations. October 23rd: 40.

272. Nasser's Status. October 28th: 26.

273. Nasser's Revolution. November 2nd: 24.

   1964

274. Nasser's Goal of "True Democracy." March 21st: 5.

275. Deepening Rift with the United States. December 2nd: 22.

276. Nasser Attacks the United States of America. December 24th: 1.

   1965

277. United States Stops Sales of Surplus Food to United Arab Republic. January 27th: 1.

278. United States Resumes Sales of Surplus Food to United Arab Republic. February 9th: 1.

279. Thirteen Years of Nasser's Rule. May 16th: Section VI, 32.

280. Ties with West Germany Broken. May 14th: 3.

281. Ties with Britain Broken. December 17th: 11.

1966

282. Nasser's Foreign and Domestic Problems. April 17th: Section IV, 7.

283. Ten Years after Suez. November 28th: 1.

1967

284. Economic Review. January 27th: 3.

285. Nasser's Economic Problems. April 28th: 2.

286. Nasser's Military Moves against Israel. May 22nd: 4.

287. War with Israel. June 5th: 1.

288. Egypt Breaks off Diplomatic Ties with the United States. June 7th: 1.

289. Nasser Resigns. June 10th: 1. Resignation Text. June 10th: 1.

290. Nasser's Failures. June 10th: 32.

291. Economic Effect of Defeat. June 11th: Section IV, 1.

292. Defeat and Nasser's Prestige. June 11th: Section IV, 1.

293. Nasser's Continuing Popularity. August 20th: Section VI, 19. October 19th: Section IV, 3.

294. Threat to Nasser's Power. October 29th: Section IV, 10.

295. Relations with Big Powers. December 3rd: Section VI, 45.

1968

296. Influence of U.S.S.R. March 29th: 40.

297. Nasser's Illness. July 25th: 8.

298. Nasser Reported as Willing to Accept Settlement with Israel. November 24th: 3.

299. Post-war Cairo. December 22nd: Section VI, 10.

1969

300. Egyptian Jews. March 2nd: 28.

301. United Arab Republic—United States Relations. April 22nd: 16.

302. Thriving Black Market. June 1st: 20.

1970

303. Economic Review. January 30th: 58.

304. Interview: Alleged United States Intentions to Overthrow Nasser. February 19th: 2.

305. World Jewish Congress Calls on Egypt to Allow the Emigration of Jews. May 11th: 3.

306. Egyptian Jews since 1967. July 29th: 16.

307. United States Views Nasser's Death as Blow to Middle East Peace Efforts. September 29th: 1.

308. Obituary. September 29th: 16.

See also:

New York Times Magazine. "Nasserism Stirs up the Middle East." (no. 92).

New York Times Magazine. "Nasser's Drives: Inside Egypt and Beyond." (no. 93).

II.   Personal Writings

Apart from his book *Egypt's Liberation: The Philosophy of the Revolution*, Nasser wrote very little. Many of his speeches are available in English. Occasional statements have been included, where appropriate, in Chapter I, section C (Periodicals and Newspapers) and section D (*The London Times* and *The New York Times*).

A. Personal Works

309. Nasser, Gamal A. *Egypt's Liberation: The Philosophy of the Revolution*. Washington, D.C.: Public Affairs Press, 1955. 119. Introduction by Thompson, Dorothy. Cairo: Government Printing Offices, 1958. 73. Buffalo, New York: Economica Books, 1959. 102. Introduction by Badeau, John S. and biographical sketch by Gunther, John.

Nasser's personal statement on the aims of Egypt's 1952 revolution. Although some doubt the book's authorship, it is nonetheless probably a true reflection of Nasser's early development in the thirties and forties. Apart from setting out the facts of his early life, the work also gives an insight into Nasser's understanding of history and power and its influence on his political consciousness. The work would help readers and researchers understand Nasser's character strengths as well as his limitations in terms of a naïve lack of political complexity.

310. Nasser, Gamal Abdel. *Nasser Speaks: Basic Documents*. Translated by Farag, E. S. London: Marssett Press, 1972. 176.

Includes *Egypt's Liberation: The Philosophy of the Revolution* and *The Charter*.

311. Nasser, Gamal Abdel. "Memoirs of the First Palestine War." *Journal of Palestine Studies*. 2 (2), Beirut: 1973. 3–32.

After Israel's raid on Gaza in 1955, Nasser wrote on his experiences in the 1948–49 war. The article sheds light on the Palestinian problem's influence on the Egyptian officers before 1952. It is an interesting insight into Nasser's psychology where a major crisis (the Gaza raid) causes regression (memories of the 1948–49 war) in order to understand the present.

312. Nasser, Gamal A. *On Non-Alignment*. Cairo: Information Administration, 1966. 34.

313. Nasser, Gamal A. *Toute la Vérité sur la Guerre de Palestine* (The Whole Truth about the Palestine War). Cairo: Direction des Relations Publiques des Forces Armees, 1955.

B. Correspondence

314. Nasser, Gamal A. and Kennedy, John F. *Lil-haqiqah wa-al-tarikh, al-mushkilah al-Filastiniyah* (also available in English: *For the Sake of Truth and for History; The Palestinian Problem*). Cairo: Information Department, 1963. 15.

The correspondence exchanged between Nasser and Kennedy on the Palestinian problem.

C. Speeches and Political Texts

There are several considerations to bear in mind when reading scripts of Nasser's speeches. There is a charisma that only comes across through listening to him. Nasser tended to dialogue with his audience thus assuming different guises according to his listeners' responses. He also used classical and colloquial Arabic. Some Arab intellectuals humorously had it that he was worth taking seriously only when he used the more formal classical Arabic. When he used the colloquial speech he was exhorting the uneducated masses. This uncharitable view has an element of truth. Nasser used classical Arabic as Shakespeare did blank verse as opposed to his prose reserved for the groundlings amongst theatre goers. Nasser himself often claimed that he "chatted" to his people rather than delivering a speech. It may be added that much of the original force is largely lost in the translation.

315. Balta, Paul and Rulleau, Claudine. *La vision nasserienne* (The Nasserist Vision). Paris: Sinbad, 1982. 279.

A collection of political texts.

316. Daumal, J. and M. Leroy. *Gamal Abd-el-Nasser avec ses textes essentiels* (Gamal Abdel Nasser and His Essential Texts). Paris: Seghers, 1967.

317. *The Islamic Pact, an Obvious Trick.* Cairo: under the auspices of the Supreme Council for Islamic Affairs, 1966. 170.

Speeches and statements by Nasser against the alliance of Islamic states led by Saudi Arabia and Iran.

318. Nasser, Gamal A. *Gamal Abd-el-Nasser.* Paris: Seghers, 1967. 191.

Texts of various speeches.

319. Nasser, Gamal A. *On the Road to African Unity; the Fourth Summit Conference, November 5, 1966.* Cairo: Ministry of National Guidance. 1966. 61.

Six speeches by Nasser.

320. Nasser, Gamal A. *Our People's Meeting with Destiny.* London: Press Office of the U.A.R. Embassy, 1962. 19.

A transcript of parts of a speech delivered on July 22nd, 1962.

321. Nasser, Gamal A. *President Gamal Abdel Nasser on Consolidation of the Cause of World Peace.* Cairo: Ministry of National Guidance, State Information Service, 1967. 350.

A collection of speeches given at international conferences and abroad. Joint communiqués with heads of state.

322. Nasser, Gamal A. *Problemy egipetskoi revoliutsii* (Problems of the Egyptian Revolution). Moscow: Mezhdunar. otnosheniia, 1979. 254.

A selection of speeches by Nasser.

323. Nasser, Gamal A. *President Gamal Abdel Nasser's Speeches and Press-Interviews*. Cairo: U.A.R. Information Office, annually during Nasser's life.

324. Nasser, Gamal A. *Speeches on the Occasion of the Thirteenth Anniversary of the Revolution, July 1965*. Cairo: Information Department, 1965. 84.

325. Nasir, Shawqi Abd al-. *Thawrat Abd al-Nasir* (Nasser's Revolution). Nicosia: Sharikat al-Mawqif al-Arabi, 1983. 718.

A selection of speeches by Nasser.

III.   General Biographies

There are several biographies of Nasser. The vast majority are written by Western biographers varying between those who are sympathetic to him and others who are overtly hostile. Hostility tends to present him as a political threat to Western nations. Later biographies have the advantage of working with a whole subject in a more comprehensive historical context. *Note*: *indicates a most useful source.

326. Agaryshev, Anatolii. *Gamal' Abdel' Naser*. Moscow: Mol. gvardiia, 1979. 208.

   Also available in a German translation by Gisela Leiste. *Gamal Abdel Nasser: Leben und Kampf eines Staatsmannes: Biografie*. (Gamal Abdel Nasser: Life and Struggle of a Statesman: Biography).

327. Ali, Shafiq Ahmad. *al-marah allati ahabbaha Abd al-Nasir* (The Woman Loved by Nasser). Cairo: Dar Nubar lil-Tiba'ah, 1989. 200.

   Giving the secrets and writings of a woman loved by Nasser. They never got married.

328. De Chancie, John. *Gamal Abdel Nasser*. New York: Chelsea House Publishers, 1988. 111.

329. Du Bois, Shirley Graham. *Gamal Abdel Nasser: Son of the Nile*. New York: The Third Press, 1972. 250.

330. Heikal, Mohammed. *Nasser: the Cairo Documents*. London: New English Library; Garden City, New York: Doubleday, 1972. 328. Reprinted with an introduction by Sheehan, Edward R. F. Garden

City, New York: Doubleday, 1973. 357. London: New English Library, 1972. 328.

Heikal was the editor of Egypt's main daily *Al-Ahram*. He later became Nasser's minister of information. This work gives an insight into Nasser's handling of other leaders. It is largely anecdotal in style.

331. *Hofstadter, Daniel (editor). *Egypt and Nasser*. New York: Facts on File, 1973. 3 volumes.

The first volume covers the early period of Nasser's leadership including his overthrow of King Farouk, the withdrawal of the British from Egypt, the unsuccessful bid for American help with the Aswan High Dam and the Suez crisis. The second volume deals with the period 1957 to 1966. The third volume deals with the 1967 Arab-Israeli War and Nasser's death.

332. *Lacouture, Jean. *Nasser*. Translated from French by Hofstadter, Daniel. London: Secker and Warburg, 1973. 394. New York: Knopf, 1973. 399.

A biography of Nasser by a sympathetic French observer with first hand experience. The narrative evokes the atmosphere of emotionalism and euphoria engendered by Nasser's leadership whilst allowing the man's limitations to speak for themselves. The biography also provides an excellent analysis of his formative years and their effects on the shaping of his policies.

333. *Mansfield, Peter. *Nasser*. London; Methuen, 1969. 217.

An impartial and well researched biography.

334. *Nutting, Anthony. *Nasser*. London: Constable, 1972. 492. One of the best biographies of Nasser written by a politician who knew him well in the fifties and the sixties. Nutting resigned from the British government over the Suez debacle.

335. St. John, Robert. *The Boss*. London: McGraw-Hill Book Company, Inc., 1960.

A rare book that reveals certain aspects of Nasser's life, e.g. family life, personal traits, children, etc. An informal biography.

336. *Stephens, Robert. *Nasser: A Political Biography*. London: Allen Lane, The Penguin Press; New York: Simon & Schuster, 1971, 631. Harmondsworth: Penguin, 1973. 635.

A comprehensive and readable biography that also analyses the political backdrops to Nasser's life.

337. United Arab Republic. *President Gamal Abdel Nasser*. Cairo: Maslahat al-Istilamat, 1965.

The official biography of Nasser.

338. Wynn, Wilton. *Nasser of Egypt: The Search for Dignity*. Cambridge: Arlington Books, 1959. 213.

A contemporary work by a journalist sympathetic to Nasser's aims and aspirations.

See also:

Little, Tom. *Egypt*. (no. 396).

Mansfield, Peter. *Nasser's Egypt*. (no. 397).

Vatikiotis, P. J. *Nasser and His Generation*. (no. 780).

IV. Background Readings

Nasser was a product of the inter-war years. The momentum driving his political life derives from events dating well back into Egypt's history. In order better to understand his life, work, and attitudes it is necessary to understand Egypt's recent history, e.g., Nasser's inherent suspicion of Western powers, the influence of Islamic fundamentalism on modern Egypt and the division within Arab ranks.

A. Egypt

339. Berger, Morroe. *Bureaucracy and Society in Modern Egypt.* Princeton: Princeton University Press, 1957. Reprinted in 1969 as *Bureaucracy and Society in Modern Egypt: A Study of the Higher Civil Service*. New York: Russell and Russell, 1969. 231.

Describes the structure and functioning of Egypt's bureaucracy and its development from the time of Muhammad Ali to independence.

340. Bilainkin, George. "Genesis of President Nasser." *Contemporary Review*. December 1962: 304+.

341. Bin Salamon, Ahmed S. *Reform of al-Azhar in the 20th Century*. Ph.D. New York University, 1980. 278. (Volume 41/06–A of *Dissertation Abstracts International*, page 2720).

Throws light on the way that Nasser decreed Law 103 and reorganised the 10th century al-Azhar into a multi-subject university with equal access to women.

342. Binder, Leonard. *In a Moment of Enthusiasm: Political Power and the Second Stratum in Egypt.* Chicago, Illinois: University of Chicago Press, 1978. 437.

A study of the political size and power of the rural middle class in Egypt. Nasser's political system is examined under the constraints of this rural middle class.

343. Blaxland, Gregory. *Objective: Egypt.* London: Frederick Muller, 1966. 319.

A narrative history of Egypt with a strong British point of view.

344. Brinton, Jasper Yeates. *The Mixed Courts of Egypt.* New Haven, Connecticut; London: Yale University Press, 1968. 297.

345. Colombe, Marcel. *L'Évolution de l'Égypte, 1924–1950* (The Evolution of Egypt: 1924–1950). Paris: Maisonneuve, 1951. 361.

A narrative survey of the history of Egypt from independence up to 1950.

346. Deeb, Marius. *Party Politics in Egypt: the Wafd and Its Rivals, 1919–1939.* London: Ithaca Press, 1979. 452.

A comprehensive analysis of Egypt's political life between the two World Wars.

347. Dodge, Bayard. *Al-Azhar: a Millennium of Muslim Learning.* Washington, D.C.: Middle East Institute, 1961. 239.

A history of al-Azhar University from 970 AD to today.

348. Dodwell, Henry. *The Founder of Modern Egypt: a Study of Muhammad Ali.* Cambridge: Cambridge University Press, reprinted 1967. 276.

Muhammad Ali ruled Egypt from 1805 to 1848 during which period he re-established political order after the recent upheavals. He laid the basis for modern Egypt.

349. Goldberg, Ellis. *Tinker, Tailor, and Textile Worker: Class and Politics in Egypt, 1930–1952.* Berkeley; Los Angeles; London: University of California Press, 1986. 220.

A study of workers and politics with an examination of the Communist Party activities in Egypt up to 1952.

350. Hinnebusch, Raymond A. "Children of the Elite: Political Attitudes of the Westernized Bourgeoisie in Contemporary Egypt." *Middle East Journal*. Volume 36, number 4, Autumn 1982, 535–61.

An insight into the Egyptian psyche that may help to explain the reasons for Nasser's partial failure in his domestic policies.

351. Holt, P. M. (editor). *Political and Social Change in Modern Egypt*. London: Oxford University Press, 1968. 400.

A collection of essays on Egyptian history from the Ottoman conquest to the present day.

352. Ibrahim. Hassan Ahmed. *The 1936 Anglo-Egyptian Treaty*. Khartoum: Khartoum University Press, 1976. 168.

A Sudanese account and analysis of the 1936 Treaty with an appendix giving the full text of the Treaty.

353. Ismail, Mahmoud Ismail Mohamed. *Nationalism in Egypt before Nasser's Revolution*. Ph.D. University of Pittsburgh, 1966. 322. (Volume 27/11-A of *Dissertation Abstracts International*, page 3908).

354. Lloyd of Dolobran, George Ambrose Lloyd, 1st Baron. *Egypt since Cromer*. New York: Macmillan, 1933–1934. Two volumes.

The author was British High Commissioner in Egypt in the 1920s. His work is an attack on British policy in Egypt. It is interesting to note that much of what he warned against did eventually lose Britain its influence in the Middle East.

355. Marsot, Afaf Lutfi al-Sayyid. *A Short History of Modern Egypt*. Cambridge: Cambridge University Press, 1985. 151.

A history covering Egypt from 639 AD to the present day.

356. Marsy, Laila. "The Military Clauses of the Anglo-Egyptian Treaty of Friendship and Alliance, 1836." *International Journal of Middle East Studies*. Volume 16, number 1, March 1984. 67–97.

The Anglo-Egyptian treaty of 1936 allowed Britain to protect its special interest in the Suez Canal whilst stating the principle of an Egypt free of foreign military occupation. This allowed Egypt a semblance of independence whilst maintaining the status quo.

357. Mayzad, A. M. H. *Ahmad Amin (Cairo 1887–1954): Advocate of Social and Literary Reform in Egypt*. Leiden, The Netherlands: Brill, 1963. 107.

Ahmad Amin is regarded as the intellectual whose influence helped to prepare the Egyptians for the 1952 Revolution.

358. McLeave, Hugh. *The Last Pharaoh: The Ten Faces of Farouk*. London, Michael Joseph, 1969. 319.

A life of Farouk with interesting insights into his dealings with the British on one hand and the Egyptian nationalists on the other.

359. Richmond, J. C. B. *Egypt 1798–1952: Her Advance towards a Modern Identity*. London: Methuen, 1977. 243.

A readable political history of Egypt from Napoleonic times to 1952.

360. Sabit, Adel M. *A King Betrayed: The Ill-Fated Reign of Farouk of Egypt*. London: Quartet Books, 1989.

A rehabilitation of King Farouk presented here as a victim of historical circumstances and a treacherous palace clique. One of the few books with a strongly hagiographic approach to the King's career.

361. Safran, Nadav. *Egypt in Search of Political Community: an Analysis of the Intellectual and Political Evolution of Egypt, 1804–1952*. Cambridge, Massachusetts: Harvard University Press, 1961. 298.

Modern Egyptian political culture is seen as formed by the traditional Islamic ideologies and liberal nationalism.

362. Shafik, Fouad Fahmy. *The Press and Politics of Modern Egypt: 1798–1970. A Comparative Analysis of Causal Relationships*. Two volumes. Ph.D. New York University, 1981. 599. (Volume 43/05–A of *Dissertation Abstracts International*, page 1672).

363. Stewart, Desmond. *Young Egypt*. London: Wingate, 1958. 198.

A book largely motivated by the author's personal experiences of the Middle East. A sympathetic history of Egypt from Napoleon to Nasser. Desmond Stewart is also the author of *Turmoil in Beirut* (London: Allan Wingate, 1958. 119.) which covers the 1958 Lebanese civil war in which Nasser was heavily implicated.

364. Terry, Janice J. *The Wafd 1919–1952: Cornerstone of Egyptian Political Power*. London: Third World Centre for Research & Publishing, 1982. 315.

A study tracing the rise and fall of the Wafd party which lasted until the revolution of 1952.

365. Vatikiotis, P. J. *The Egyptian Army in Politics: Pattern for New Nations*. Bloomington, Indiana: Indiana University Press, 1961. 261.

A study of the conditions that brought military groups into political power in the Middle East with particular reference to Egypt as a case study.

366. Vatikiotis, P. J. *The History of Egypt*. London: Weidenfeld and Nicolson; Baltimore, Maryland: John Hopkins University Press, 1986. 560.

This book was originally published as *The Modern History of Egypt: The History of Egypt from Mohammad Ali to Sadat*.

367. Vatikiotis, P. J. *The Modern History of Egypt*. New York: Praeger, 1969. 512.

This work covers Egypt's internal affairs in a way that seeks to explain much of Nasser's subsequent era. Arab socialism is seen as resting on established trends in Egyptian society.

368. Warburg, Gabriel R. "Egypt's Regional Policy from Muhammad Ali to Muhammad Anwar al-Sadat." *The Contemporary Mediterranean World*. Edited by Pinkele, Carl F. and Pollis, Adamantia. New York: Praeger, 1983. 124–50.

Egypt's regional policy during the 19th and 20th centuries.

369. Waterfield, Gordon. *Egypt*. London: Thames and Hudson; New York: Walker and Company, 1967. 230.

A history of Egypt from ancient times to Nasser. Its primary aim is to remove ostensible Western misconceptions about Egypt.

370. Wendell, Charles. *The Evolution of the Egyptian National Image from Its Origins to Ahmad Lutfi al-Sayyid*. Berkeley, California: University of California Press, 1972. 313.

A discussion of the concept of Islamic umma (political community) and its clash with the concept of Egyptian nationhood.

371. Whittington, Dale. *Water Management in Egypt: A Case Study of the Aswan High Dam*. Ph.D. The University of Texas at Austin, 1980. (Volume 42/11–B of *Dissertation Abstracts International*, page 4554).

See also

Abo-El-Enein, Mohammed Mahmoud. *The State, Dominant Class Segments, and Capital Accumulation in Egypt since 1805, with Special Reference to the "Open Door" Élite of 1974–1986*. (no. 794).

B. The Middle East

372. Antonius, George. *The Arab Awakening: The Story of the Arab National Movement*. Beirut: Librairie du Liban, 1969. 471.

First published in 1938 this is a seminal work on the Arab world and its newly found nationalism.

373. Secretariat of the Asian-African Legal Consultative Committee in New Delhi. *Constitutions of African States*. New York: Oceana Publications. 1972. Two volumes.

Volume 2 includes a summary of constitutional developments in Egypt. 1691+.

374. Binder, Leonard. *The Ideological Revolution in the Middle East*. New York: John Wiley, 1964. 287.

On the ideological foundations of Egyptian-Arab nationalism and Nasserism.

375. Bonne, Alfred. *The Economic Development of the Middle East: An Outline of Planned Reconstruction after the War*. New York: Oxford University Press, 1945. 164.

The work covers Egypt amongst other countries.

376. Kimche, Jon. *The Second Arab Awakening: The Middle East 1914–1970*. New York: Holt, Rinehart and Winston, 1970.

C. Israel and Palestine

377. Jeffries, Joseph Mary Nagle. *Palestine: The Reality*. New York: Longmans, 1939. 728.

A comprehensive scholarly work on the British handling of the Palestinian mandate.

378. Laqueur, Walter (editor). *The Israel-Arab Reader*. London: Pelican Books, 1970. 591.

A comprehensive documentary history of the Arab-Israeli conflict.

379. Shipler, David K. *Arab and Jew: Wounded Spirits in a Promised Land*. London: Bloomsbury Publishing Ltd., 1986. 596.

This work explores the relationship between Arab and Jew giving an insight into the personal psychology of the conflict.

See also:

Colonial Office. *CO 537 Palestine Files*. (no. 19).

Colonial Office. *CO 733 Palestine Corrspondence*. (no. 20).

D. Fiction

380. Sheehan, Edward R. F. *Kingdom of Illusion*. Panther, 1967.

Although a fictional work, it is based on real events between 1952 and 1956. More importantly, the work conveys the spirit of the times and the events involving Nasser.

V.   Youth and Rise to Power

The following list does not include biographies already listed in section III above.

A. General

381. al-Baraway, Rashid. *The Military Coup in Egypt, 1952*. Cairo: Renaissance Bookshop, 1952. Westport, Connecticut, 1981. 269.

   The book seeks to prove that the 1952 revolution was a social necessity born from various inter-related forces. It includes an interesting section on the revolution's major reforms.

382. Childers, Erskine. "Nasser's Egypt: the First Decade since the Revolution." *Listener*. November 15th 1962: 795+.

383. Falls, Cyril. "Colonel Nasser." *Illustrated London News*. March 16th 1957: 414+.

384. Gordon, Joel S. *Towards Nasser's Egypt: The Consolidation of the July Revolution and the End of the Old Régime, 1952–1955*. Two volumes. Ph.D. the University of Michigan, 1987. 552. (Volume 48/06-A of *Dissertation Abstracts International*, page 1524.)

385. Jankowski, James P. *Egypt's Young Rebels: 'Young Egypt,' 1933–1952*. Stanford, California: Hoover Institution Press, 1975. 154.

A study of the Young Egypt Society which, though short lived, continued to operate under different guises until 1952.

386. Joesten, Joachim. *Nasser: The Rise to Power*. London: Odhams Press, 1960. 224. Westport, Connecticut: Greenwood Press, 1974. 224.

A critical biography of Nasser.

387. Karanjia, Rustom Khurshedji. *How Nasser Did It*. Bombay: Jaico Publishing House, 1964. 146.

On Nasser's revolution and its aftermath.

388. Laqueur, Walter. *Nasser's Egypt*. London: Weidenfeld and Nicholson, 1956. 31.

389. Robbe, Martin and Hosel, Jurgen (editors). *Egypt: The Revolution of July 1952 and Gamal Abdel Nasser*. Berlin-D.D.R.: Akademie-Verlag, 1989. 130.

390. Sadat, Anwar. *Revolt on the Nile*. London: Allan Wingate; New York: John Day Company, 1957. 159.

Anwar Sadat describes his role in the 1952 revolution. With a forward by Nasser.

391. Wheelock, Keith. *Nasser's New Egypt: A Critical Analysis*. London: Stevens & Sons; New York: Praeger, 1960. 326.

Various aspects of Nasser's government are critically reviewed, these including economics, industrialization, the Aswan High Dam and education. Nasserism is seen as a purely Egyptian movement devoid of any real commitment to Arab ideology. It is an interesting book written with Nasser's co-operation in facilitating the author's work.

B. Wider Political Context

392. Botman, Selma. "The Egyptian Communist Movement in Perspective." *Journal of South Asian and Middle Eastern Studies*. Volume 10, number 3, Spring 1987, 78–94.

An article covering Egypt in the 20th century. It contrasts three distinct periods of modern Egypt: (1) the 1920s, (2) up to 1952 and (3) under Nasser's leadership.

393. Botman, Selma. "Egyptian Communists and the Free Officers, 1950–54." *Middle Eastern Studies*. London, 22 (3), 1986: 350–366.

On Nasser's use and treatments of the Communists.

394. Botman, Selma. *Oppositional Politics in Egypt: The Communist Movement, 1939–1954*. Ph.D. Harvard University. 1984. 594. (Volume 45/07–A of *Dissertation Abstracts International*, page 2223).

Showing the two phases of the development of Communism in Egypt. Communism was essentially a European concept adopted by Greeks, Italians and Jews living in Egypt. Later on it was propagated by students and intellectuals. Nasser's regime was trenchantly anti-Communist.

395. Haddad, George M. *Revolutions and Military Rule in the Middle East: Egypt, the Sudan, Yemen, and Libya*. New York: Robert Speller, 1973. 444.

Dealing with the conditions in Egypt that led to the 1952 revolution and its immediate aftermath. Also analysed are Nasser and Nasserism.

396. Little, Tom. *Egypt*. London: Ernest Benn, 1958. 334.

History of Egypt covering the rise of nationalism under British rule on to Nasser's early years in power. The work was later updated (see number 642 below).

397. Mansfield, Peter. *Nasser's Egypt*. Harmondsworth, England; Baltimore, Maryland: Penguin Books, 1965. 222.

A readable book by Nasser's biographer which deals with the first ten years of Nasser's rule.

398. Mikhailo, A. "An Important Milestone in Egypt's History." *International Affairs* (U.S.S.R.), (8), 1977. 46–53.

A review of Egypt's struggle for independence after 1952.

399. Neguib, Mohammed. *Egypt's Destiny*. London: Victor Gollancz, 1955. 273.

An account of the revolution by Neguib who was the first prime minister from 1952 until 1954.

400. Royal Institute of International Affairs. *Great Britain and Egypt, 1914–1951*. Information Papers, number 19. 1952. 210.

Based largely on official documents and press reports this is a British point of view of what happened in Egypt during the first half of the 20th century.

See also:

McLeave, Hugh. *The Last Pharaoh: The Ten Faces of Farouk.* (no. 358).

Sabit, Adel M. *A King Betrayed: The Ill-Fated Reign of Farouk of Egypt.* (no. 360).

VI. Approaches to the West

Nasser's foreign policy vis à vis the West was partly planned and partly reactive to events. He was not averse to playing the superpowers one off against the others when the opportunity presented itself. In many cases events overtook him thus scuttling some of his earlier planning.

A. Britain, the United States and the Western World

401. Abdul Fath, Ahmed. *L'Affaire Nasser* (The Nasser Affair). Paris: Plon, 1962.

402. Aronson, Geoffrey. *From Sideshow to Center Stage: U.S. Policy towards Egypt, 1946–1956*. Boulder, Colorado: Lynne Rienner, 1986. 208.

Covering the ten years after the Second World War and analysing the U.S. failure to achieve its policy goals.

403. Badeau, John. *The American Approach to the Arab World*. Council on Foreign Relations, Harper and Row, 1968.

404. Brinton, Jasper Yeates. *The American Effort in Egypt: A Chapter in Diplomatic History in the Nineteenth Century*. Alexandria, Egypt: Imprimerie du Commerce, 1972. 147.

Written by an American who lived in Egypt for fifty years.

405. Brown, Donald S. "Egypt and the United States: Collaborators in Economic Development." *Middle East Journal*, volume 35, number 1, Winter 1981, 3–14.

406. Bumbacher, Beat. *Die USA und Nasser: amerikanische Agypten—
   Politik der Kennedy und Johnson Amninistration, 1961-1967* (The
   U.S.A. and Nasser: American-Egyptian Politics of the Kennedy and
   Johnson Administrations). Stuttgart: F. Steiner Verlag Wiesbaden,
   1987. 308.

407. Burns, William J. *"The Carrot and the Stick": Economic Aid and
   American Policy Towards Egypt, 1955–1967*. Ph.D. University of
   Oxford. 1981. 329. (Volume 49/08–A of *Dissertation Abstracts
   International*, page 2381).

A study which shows how American aid to Egypt failed in exerting
influence on Egyptian affairs. Nasser was particularly averse to any hint
that Egyptian dependence on American aid gave the U.S. control over
Egyptian foreign policy. An interesting study in terms of current U.S.-
Arab relations seemingly going the same way. The work was later updated
and published (see number 408 below).

408. Burns, Williams J. *Economic Aid and American Policy towards
   Egypt, 1955–1981*. New York: State University of New York Press,
   1985. 285.

After Egypt's first arms deal with the Communist Bloc, the United
States sought to influence Nasser's foreign policy through its aid programme. The plan was to make Nasser support United States interest in
the Middle East and cease his reliance on Soviet help. This book shows
how this policy fared under Nasser and Sadat.

409. Childers, E. B. *The Road to Suez: A Study of Western-Arab Relations*. London: MacGibbon and Kee, 1962.

410. Copeland, Miles. *The Game of Nations*. New York: Simon and
   Schuster, 1970. 318.

A work that analyses the strategy of international power politics as
experienced by the author's first hand knowledge of Nasser's relations
with the United States.

411. Crabites, Pierre. *Americans in the Egyptian Army*. London: George
   Routledge, 1938. 277.

Egypt hired American officers in the 1870s. This book presents some
of their achievements. (See no. 415 below).

412. DeNovo, John A. "The Eisenhower Doctrine." In Alexander De Conde (editor), *Encyclopedia of American Foreign Policy*. New York: Scribner's, 1978. Volume 1, 292–301.

413. Genco, Stephen J. "The Eisenhower Doctrine: Deterrence in the Middle East, 1957–1958." In Alexander George and Richard Smoke, *Deterrence in American Foreign Policy: Theory and Practice*. New York: Columbia University Press, 1974, 309–362.

414. Hammudah, Adil. *al-hurub al-khafiyah ma al-mukhabarat al—Amerikiyah* (Wars with the American Intelligence). Cairo: al-Dar al-Arabiyah, 1989. 444.

415. Hassetine, William B. *The Blue and The Gray on the Nile*. Chicago, Illinois: University of Chicago Press; Toronto: University of Toronto Press, 1961. 290.

An account of the fifty American West Point graduates hired by the Khedive Ismail in the 1870s. (See no. 411 above).

416. Jabber, Paul. "Egypt's Crisis, America's Dilemma." *Foreign Affairs*, volume 64, issue 5, Summer 1986: 960–980.

Egypt's economico-political development traced from Nasser's time onwards concluding on the steps the United States needs to take.

417. Al-Jebarin, Abdulqadir Ismail. *The United States-Egyptian Relations, 1945–1958*. D.A. Illinois State University, 1988. 272. (Volume 49/08–A of *Dissertation Abstracts International*, pages 2363).

Showing how American foreign policy under Truman and Eisenhower attempted to enhance U.S. influence in the region. Its reaction to events rather than having a long term cohesive policy, its support of Israel and its misunderstanding of Arab nationalism doomed American policy to failure.

418. Johnson, Lyndon Baines. *The Vantage Point: Perspectives of the Presidency 1963–1969*. London, 1972.

419. Khrunov, Evgenil. "Race to Help Nasser." *U.S. News and World Report*, volume 56, June 8th 1964: 70+.

On economic aid to Nasser's Egypt.

420. Lenczowski, George. "New Dimensions of Big-power Rivalry in the Middle East." *The Contemporary Mediterranean World*. Edited

by Pinkele, Carl F. and Pollis, Adamantia. New York: Praeger, 1983: 32–49.

A review of the relationship between the super powers and the Middle East.

421. Little, Douglas. "The New Frontier on the Nile: JFK, Nasser and Arab Nationalism." *Journal of American History*, volume 75, issue 2, September 1988: 501–527.

Kennedy's failed attempts at establishing a lasting rapprochement with Egypt are carefully examined.

422. Mansfield, Peter. *The British in Egypt.* London: Weidenfeld & Nicolson; New York: Holt, Rinehart and Winston, 1971. 351.

An account of the British occupation of Egypt from 1882 to 1954. It is seen as "in many ways neither a happy one nor one of which Englishmen can be especially proud." It seeks to explain the importance of Egypt to the West and the Egyptian's seeming servility.

423. Marlowe, John. *Anglo-Egyptian Relations (1800–1956).* London: Frank Cass, 1965. 432.

Discusses the relationship between Britain and Muhammad Ali, the Suez Canal, the British rule of Egypt and the Sudan and the role of Cromer. An assessment is made of the British occupation of Egypt and its strategic importance, the 1952 revolution and the Suez War.

424. Marlowe, John. *Perfidious Albion: The Origins of Anglo-French Rivalry in the Levant.* London: Elek Books, 1971. 323.

Despite its title, this work is concerned mainly with the history of Britain's imposed settlement in Egypt.

425. Mayer, Gail F. *Egypt and the United States: the Formative Years.* Teaneck, New Jersey: Fairleigh Dickinson University Press, 1980. 230.

Covering the period 1952–1958.

426. Monroe, Elizabeth. *Britain's Moment in the Middle East, 1914–1956.* Baltimore: John Hopkins Press, 1963. 254.

Based on the thesis that British presence in the Middle East was purely extra-regional in its aims, this work analyses Britain's failure in the Islamic world.

427. Nadelmann, Ethan. "Setting the Stage: American Policy towards the Middle East, 1961–1966." *International Journal of Middle East Studies*, volume 14, issue 4, November 1982. 435–457.

Shows how the United States tried to maintain a regional balance whilst failing to respond to Egyptian initiatives or doing so belatedly.

428. Patterson, Thomas G. *American Foreign Policy: A History.* Lexington, Massachusetts: D. C. Heath & Company, 1977. 607.

Short entries on the Middle East 506+ and 586+.

429. Rubin, Barry. "America and the Egyptian Revolution, 1950–1957." *Political Science Quarterly*, volume 97, issue 1, Spring 1982. 73–90.

Shows how Nasser turned from potential U.S. ally to foe as the Americans continually misunderstood his drive for self-assertion.

430. Speiser, Ephraim Avigdor. *The United States and the Near East.* Cambridge: Harvard University Press, revised edition, 1950. 283.

Although the work predates Nasser's rule, it is an authoritative and informed analysis of American policy in the Middle East. Despite its title, the work gives brilliant analyses of Zionism, Arab Nationalism and British imperialism.

431. Spiegel, Steven L. *The Middle East and the Western Alliance.* London; Boston, Massachusetts: Allen & Unwin, 1982. 256.

A discussion of the Arab-Israeli conflict, the energy crisis and Middle Eastern instability in the light of superpower interests.

432. Speigel, Steven L. *The Other Arab-Israeli Conflict: Making America's Middle East Policy, from Truman to Reagan.* Chicago: The University of Chicago Press, 1985. 522.

433. Stevens, Georgiana G. "1967–1977: America's Moment in the Middle East?" *Middle East Journal.* 31:1, 1977: 1–15.

A representation of America's so-called "overriding aim" of preventing Soviet dominance in the Middle East.

434. Tansky, Leo. *U.S. and U.S.S.R. Aid to Developing Countries: a Comparative Study of India, Turkey and U.A.R.* New York: Praeger, 1967. 192.

A study of the purpose and achievements of Soviet and American aid to India, Turkey and Egypt.

435. Tibawi, A. L. *Anglo-Arab Relations*. London: Luzac, 1978.

436. Weinbaum, Marvin G. *Egypt and the Politics of U.S. Economic Aid*. Boulder, Colorado; London: Westview Press, 1986. 192.

437. Wilson, Keith M. (editor). *Imperialism and Nationalism in the Middle East*. London: Mansell Publishing Limited, 1983. 172.

A collection of papers, the majority of which were delivered during a symposium held at the University of Leeds in 1981. These papers analyse the Anglo-Egyptian relationship in terms of politics, trade, diplomacy and nationalism. Although the issues discussed are complex, the papers are very readable.

See also:

Foreign Office. *FO 406*. (no. 21).

Foreign Office. *FO 891*. (no. 26).

Selim, Mohammed El-Sayed. *The Operational Code Belief System and Foreign Policy Decision Making: The Case of Gamal Abdel-Nasser*. (no. 806).

Numbers 5–7 and 9–16 in chapter I, section A above.

B. The Soviet Union

438. Abu-Jaber, Faiz S. "The Soviets and the Arabs: 1917–1955." *Middle East Forum*, volume 45, number 1, 1969. 13–44.

Discusses topics such as the Soviet-Egyptian opposition to the Middle East Defence Organization, Soviet-Egyptian trade, Non-Alignment and Afro-Asian politics.

439. Abu-Jaber, Faiz S. "The Soviet Attitude toward Arab Revolutions: Yemen, Egypt, Algeria, Iraq and Palestine." *Middle East Forum*, volume 46, number 4, 1970. 41–65.

440. Dawisha, Karen. *Soviet Foreign Policy towards Egypt*. London: Macmillan, 1979. 271.

A very good study of the developments in Soviet-Egyptian relations between 1955 and 1978.

441. Heikal, Mohamed. *Sphinx and Commisar: The Rise and Fall of Soviet Influence in the Arab World.* London: Collins, 1978. 303.

Heikal was Nasser's closest friend and political ally. Present at most of the major decisions taken by Nasser, Heikal is in a unique position to give this vivid account of how Nasser dealt with Russia.

442. Hirschmann, Ira. *Red Star over Bethlehem.* New York: Simon and Schuster, 1971. 192.

A work analysing Russia's attempt to "capture" the Middle East. It has special reference to Nasser.

443. el Hussini, Mohrez Mahmoud. *Soviet-Egyptian Relations, 1945–1985.* London: Macmillan Press, 1987. 260.

Written largely from the viewpoint of the Egyptian navy.

444. Laqueur, Walter Z. *The Soviet Union and the Middle East.* New York: Praeger, 1959. 366.

A country by country survey of Soviet policy in the Middle East.

445. Laqueur, Walter Z. *The Struggle for the Middle East: The Soviet Union in the Mediterranean, 1958–1968.* New York: Macmillan, 1969. 360.

A follow-up of Laqueur's *The Soviet Union and the Middle East* which analyses Soviet policy in the sixties showing it at its most active and successful.

446. Lenczowski, George. *Soviet Advances in the Middle East.* Washington, D.C.: American Enterprise Institute for Public Policy Research, 1972. 176.

One chapter (pages 77–102) on Soviet-Egyptian relations between 1959 and 1972.

447. Sabry, Aly. "Tension: Nasser and the Russians." *Newsweek Magazine*, volume 74, October 6th 1969. 74+.

An article by Nasser's Prime Minister (1964–5) and Chairperson of the Arab Socialist Union.

See also:

Beinin, Joel. "The Communist Movement and Nationalist Political Discourse in Nasirist Egypt." (no. 580).

Botman, Selma. "The Egyptian Communist Movement in Perspective." (no. 392).

Botman, Selma. "Egyptian Communists and the Free Officers, 1950–54." (no. 393).

Botman, Selma. *Oppositional Politics in Egypt: The Communist Movement, 1939–1954*. (no. 394).

Laqueur, Walter Z. "Nasser and the Iraqi Communists." (no. 639).

Laqueur, Walter Z. *Communism and Nationalism in the Middle East*. (no. 638).

C. Other Nations

448. Egyptian Society of International Law. *Egypt and the United Nations: Report of a Study Group Set up by the Egyptian Society of International Law*. New York: Manhattan Publishing Company, 1957. 197.

449. Fabunmi, L. A. *The Sudan in Anglo-Egyptian Relations*. New York: Longmans, 1960. 466.

A work that argues the case for unity of the Nile valley.

450. Nasser-Eddine, Mon'im. *Arab-Chinese Relations, 1950–1971*. Beirut: Arab Institute for Research and Publishing. 322.

Despite the title this is a work concerned only with Egyptian-Chinese relations.

See also Chapter IX, section B.

VII.   Suez

There is a huge amount written on Suez. The following is a limited list including as many participants' points of view as possible. Naturally, titles under each section below overlap somewhat.

A. Suez up to Nationalization

451. Azeau, H. *Le Piège de Suez (5 novembre 1956)*(The Suez Trap). Paris: Robert Laffont, 1964.

452. Cansacchi, G. "A Challenge to Law. Colonel Nasser and the Suez Canal." *Round Table 184*, 1956. 307–311.

453. Charles-Roux, F. "Le blocage du canal du Suez" (The Suez Blockage). *Comptes Rendus, Académie des Sciences Morales et Politiques*, November 1956.

454. Charles-Roux, F. "Le coup de force du gouvernement égyptiene contre la Compagnie Universelle du Canal Maritime de Suez" (The Egyptian Government's Use of Force against the Universal Company of the Suez Maritime Canal). *Revue des Travaux de l'Académie de Sciences Morales et Politiques*, 1956. 141–154.

455. Charles-Roux, F. "Le coup de Suez" (The Suez Coup). *Revue de Paris*, October 1956.

456. Childers, Erskine B. *The Road to Suez*. London: MacGibbon and Kee, 1962. 416.

A readable and intelligent study of Western-Arab relations seen through Suez. Much of the work is written from a point of view sympathetic to Arabs showing why Western policies in the Middle East have constantly gone wrong—at their worst reaching the Suez debacle.

457. Connell, J. *The Most Important Country: The True Story of the Suez Crisis and the Events Leading to It.* London: Cassell, 1957.

458. Eban, A. S. "Freedom of Navigation through the Suez Canal. The Israeli-Egyptian Dispute Discussed by a Legal Correspondent." *Petroleum Times*, September 1955. 911–915.

459. Egypt, Ministry for Foreign Affairs. *White Paper on the Nationalisation of the Suez Maritime Canal Company.* Cairo: Government Press, 1956.

460. Fahmy-Abdou, A. *La nazionalizzazione della Societa del Canale di Suez* (The Nationalisation of the Suez Canal Company). Cairo: Mondiale, 1962.

461. Farnie, D. A. *East and West of Suez: The Suez Canal in History.* Oxford: Clarendon Press, 1969. 860.

A scholarly and definitive work on the subject. Part Four gives a history of British involvement in the Middle East. Part Five relates recent history up to the 1956 Suez War.

462. Georges-Picot, Jacques. *The Real Suez Crisis: The End of a Great Nineteenth Century Work.* Translated from the French by Rogers, W. G. New York; London: Harcourt Brace Jovanovich, 1978. 200.

First published in French in 1975 (Paris: Editions de la R.P.P.). Covering Egypt's political evolution leading up to the crisis. Also analysed are the Company's attitude to, and the crisis itself. Largely seen through the eyes of the Compagnie Universelle du Canal Maritime de Suez of which the author was the general manager.

463. Ghobashy, O. Z. "The Suez Canal Convention of 1888." *Revue Égyptienne de Droit International*, 12. 1956. 28–51.

464. Henriques, Robert. *One Hundred Hours to Suez: An Account of Israel's Campaign in the Sinai Peninsula.* London: Collins, 1957. 254.

A strongly pro-Israeli analysis of Suez in particular and the Arab-Israeli conflict in general.

465. Israel, Ministry for Foreign Affairs. *Egypt and the Suez Canal, 1948–1956; a Record of Lawlessness.* Jerusalem: Ministry Publication, 1956.

466. Kipping, Sir Norman. *The Suez Contractors.* Havant, England: Kenneth Mason Publications, 1969. 80.

Between 1954 and 1956 the British conceived and carried out a plan for the withdrawal of their forces in the Suez Canal zone. The maintenance and operation of the Canal was to be handed over to civilians. This short book traces the history of this policy.

467. Lawrence, E. V. *Egypt and the West: Salient Facts behind the Suez Crisis.* New York: American Institute of International Information, 1956. 85.

Analyses the Suez crisis as being a result of Soviet penetration into the Middle East threatening Western interests.

468. Lunz, L. A. "Die Nationalisierung der Suez-Kanal-Gesellschaft ist ein souveranes Recht Agyptens." (The Nationalisation of the Suez Canal Company Is a Sovereign Right of Egypt). *Rechtswissenschaftlicer Informationsdienst* (Legal Information Service). 1958: 247–254.

469. Luthy, H. and Rodnick, D. *French Motivations in the Suez Crisis.* Princeton: Institute for International Social Research, 1956.

470. Nousier, A. and Moonis, H. *The Suez Canal. Facts and Documents.* Cairo: Selected Studies No. 5, 1956.

471. Obeita, Joseph A. *The International Status of the Suez Canal.* The Hague: Martinus Nijhoff, 1970. 154.

The author argues that the concession of 1856 imposes upon Egypt a legal duty to afford free passage to all merchant ships in time of peace.

472. Olmstead, C. J. "International Law: Nationalization of the Suez Canal." *Annual Survey of American Law*, 1956. 1–23.

473. Scelle, G. "La nationalisation du canal de Suez et le droit international" (The Nationalisation of Suez and International Law). *Annuaire Francais de Droit International*, 2. 1956. 3–19.

474. Schonfield, Hugh J. *The Suez Canal*. Harmondsworth: Penguin, 1939. 179.

An interesting British view of the Canal and its history. The book also includes the original Firman of Concession granted to Lesseps by the Viceroy of Egypt and a copy of the International Convention of 1888 signed in Constantinople by the European powers, Russia and Turkey.

475. Al-Solami, Dawi Awaad. *British Preparations for the Suez War*. Ph.D. Exeter: University of Exeter, 1988. 397. (Volume 50/03–A of *Dissertation Abstracts International*, page 777).

Showing how Britain prepared with the aim of overthrowing Nasser and establishing a friendly régime in Egypt. The study shows a catalogue of failures, divisions, miscalculations and fear of Soviet involvement all of which lost Britain its ultimate goal.

476. Suez Canal Company. *The Suez Canal Company and the Decision Taken by the Egyptian Government on 26 July, 1956*. Paris: Imprimerie S.E.F., 1956. Two volumes.

477. United Kingdom. *Exchange of Correspondence between the Suez Committee and the President of the Republic of Egypt Regarding the Future Operation of the Suez Canal*. Cairo: September 3–9. Egypt No. 2. Cmd. 9856, London: HMSO, 1956.

478. United States, Department of State. *The Suez Canal Problem, July 26-September 22, 1956. A Documentary Publication*. Washington, D.C.: Department of State Publication 6392, 1956.

479. Watt, D. C. *Documents of the Suez Crisis, 26 July to 6 November 1956*. London: Royal Institute of International Affairs, 1957.

480. Wilson, Arnold T. *The Suez Canal: Its Past, Present, and Future*. London: Oxford University Press, 1939. 224.

A scholarly study including several key documents in its appendices.

481. Wint, Guy and Calvocoressi, Peter. *Middle East Crisis*. Harmondsworth: Penguin, 1957. 141.

A contemporary step by step account of the Suez War with some appendices: Tripartite Declaration, 25 May 1950, Security Council Resolution, 13 October 1956, and letter from Hammarskjold to Fawzi, 24 October 1956.

482. Zimmerman, John. "The Origins of the Fedayeen in Nasser's Weltpolitik: Prelude to the Suez War." *Historian*, 42 (1), 1979. 101–118.

An article showing how Nasser allegedly used the fedayeen as paid saboteurs against Israel in an attempt to achieve his Pan-Arab policies.

See also:

Childers, E. B. *The Road to Suez: A Study of Western-Arab Relations*. (no. 409).

U.S. Department of State. *The Suez Canal Problem: July 26–September 22, 1956: A Documentary Publication. (no. 13)*.

B. The Suez War

483. Barker, A. J. *Suez: The Seven Day War*. London: Faber and Faber, 1964. 223.

A somewhat partisan work showing Britain's point of view. Written by an ex-military man, it deals mainly with the military aspects of the invasion and, briefly, with its consequences to British military strategy.

484. Bastid, S. "L'action militaire franco-britannique et le droit des Nations Unies" (The Franco-British Military Action and United Nations Law). *Mélanges Gidel*, Paris, Sirey, 1961.

485. Beaufre, A. *The Suez Expedition*, 1956. London: Faber and Faber, 1969.

486. Beloff, M. "Suez and the British Conscience. A Personal Report." *Commentary*, 23 (4), 1957. 309–315.

487. Benton, W. E. "United Nations' Action in the Suez Crisis." *International Law and the Middle East Crisis: A Symposium*, Tulane University, 1957. 5–23.

488. Bromberger, Merry and Serge. *Secrets of Suez*. Translated from the French by Cameron, James. London: Pan Books, 1957. 192.

A work giving a defence of France and its allies' behaviour during the Suez War. At the time of its appearance it caused a sensation by its description of what the authors saw as a worthy operation wholly mismanaged.

489. Byford-Jones, W. *Oil on Troubled Waters*. London: Robert Hale
     Limited, 1957. 255.

A book on Suez seen from a British point of view with a strong
anti-Egyptian stance. It includes the text of Nasser's speech on the nationalization of the Suez Canal Company delivered in Alexandria on July
26, 1956.

490. Carlton, David. *Britain and the Suez Crisis*. London: Basil Black-
     well, 1988. 174.

The Suez Crisis seen through British eyes with a readable background
on the main personalities involved.

491. Dayan, Moshe. *Diary of the Sinai Campaign*. London: Weidenfeld
     and Nicolson, 1966. 236.

An Israeli general's eyeview of Suez.

492. Dumont, C. and Lepleux, P. "L'affaire de Suez" (The Suez Affair).
     Les Cahiers de L'Orient Contemporain, 1956. 36–101.

493. Eban, A. S. "Sinai and Suez—A Retrospect." *Voice of Israel*,
     London: Faber, 1958. 236–248.

494. Eden, Anthony. *The Memoirs of Anthony Eden*: Volume I, *Full
     Circle*. London: Cassell, 1960.

Eden's account of the 1956 Suez War. Gives an insight into Eden's
perception of Nasser.

495. Eden, A. *The Suez Crisis of 1956*. Boston: Beacon Press, 1968.

496. Fawzi, Mahmoud. *Suez 1956: An Egyptian Perspective*. London:
     Shorouk International, 1986. 149.

An Egyptian history written by the then Foreign Minister of Egypt.

497. Fullick, Roy and Powell, Geoffrey. *Suez: The Double War*. London:
     Hamish Hamilton, 1979. 227.

Details the political and diplomatic intrigues as experienced by the
authors in 1956.

498. Heikal, Mohamed H. *Cutting the Lion's Tail: Suez through Egyptian
     Eyes*. London: Andre Deutsch, 1986. 238.

Heikal, as a close friend and confidant of Nasser's, is well placed to write this first-hand account. Although somewhat partisan it makes interesting reading particularly in understanding Nasser the man.

499. Hennessy, Peter. "Through Egyptian Eyes." *New Statesman*, volume 112, November 14th 1986. 21+.

Suez from Egypt's point of view.

500. Hourani, A. H. *The Middle East and the Crisis of 1956*. St. Antony's Papers, number 4, *Middle Eastern Affairs*, number 1, London: Chatto, 1958.

501. Hugh, Thomas. *Suez*. New York: Harper and Row, 1967. 261.

An almost day by day narration covering three months of the crisis.

502. Johnson, Paul. *The Suez War*. London: MacGibbon & Kee, 1957. 145.

A critical analysis of the tripartite attack on Egypt. With a foreward by Aneurin Bevan (Minister in the Attlee Government). Amongst other things it seeks to explain Suez in terms of the Tories' 'Munich psychosis' forcing Eden to embark on a disastrous road.

503. Lloyd, Selwyn. *Suez 1956: A Personal Account*. London: Jonathan Cape, 1978. 282.

Conservative Secretary of State for Foreign Affairs recounts his personal experiences and perceptions of Suez. The book is worth reading as a foil to Anthony Nuttings's *No End of a Lesson: The Story of Suez* (see number 507 below).

504. Love, Kennett. *Suez: The Twice-Fought War*. New York; Toronto: McGraw-Hill, 1969. 767.

A detailed study of the Suez War with a short final section on the 1967 Arab-Israeli War seen as a repeat of 1956 with main differences highlighted.

505. Neff, Donald. *Warriors at Suez*. New York: Simon & Schuster, 1981. 479.

Written by a journalist, the work seeks to show the end of France and Britain as world powers as a result of the Suez War. Each chapter presents the story from a participant's point of view.

506. Nimer, B. "Dulles, Suez and Democratic Diplomacy." *Western Political Quarterly*, 1959. 784–798.

507. Nutting, A. *No End of a Lesson: The Story of Suez*. London: Constable, 1967.

A critical analysis by a junior minister in Eden's government of Britain's involvement in the Suez War. An opposing point of view may be read in Selwyn Lloyd's *Suez 1956: A Personal Account* (see number 503 above). Nutting resigned his office over Suez. This account is followed by useful appendices of relevant documents.

508. O'Ballance, Edgar. *The Sinai Campaign 1956*. London: Faber and Faber, 1959. 223.

A narrative of the Israeli military strike into Egypt during the Suez War, with a strong Israeli bias.

509. Syracuse. *Middle East in Crisis: A Historical and Documentary Review*. Syracuse, New York: Syracuse University Press, 1959. 213.

Analysis supported by 48 documents and speeches.

510. Ulloa, A. "El conflicto del canal de Suez" (The Suez Canal Conflict). *Rivista peruana de Derecho Internacional*, 50, 1956. 3–60.

See also:

United States Department of State. *Suez Canal Crisis, July 27–December 31, 1956*. (no. 12).

United States Department of State. *United States Policy in the Middle East: September 1956–June 1957, Documents*. (no. 14).

C. After Suez

511. Adams, M. *Suez and after. Year of Crisis*. Boston: Beacon, 1958.

512. Allaun, F. *The Cost of Suez*. London: Union of Democratic Control, 1957.

513. *American Journal of International Law*. "Egypt: Declaration on the Suez Canal," 51, 1957. 673–675.

514. American Society of International Law. *International Law and the Middle East Crisis*. New Orleans: Tulane University Press, 1957.

515. Arias, Y. S. "L'aspect juridique de la question de Suez" (The Legal Aspect of the Suez Question). *Les Cahiers de l'Europe Naissante*, volume 2. Modena: Societa Tipografica Editrice Modenese.

516. Arias, Y. S. *El Canal de Suez. Aspecto historico, juridico, politico y economico* (The Suez Canal. Historical, Legal, Political and Economical Aspects). Universidad de Concepcion, 1958.

517. Atyeo, H. C. "Egypt since the Suez Crisis." *Middle Eastern Affairs*, June 1958.

518. Badr, G. M. "Israel and the Suez Canal: A New Approach." *Revue Égyptienne de Droit International*, 17. 1961. 103–130.

519. Braddon, Russell. *Suez: Splitting of a Nation.* London: Collins. 1973. 253.

The Suez crisis explored through related political dimensions, e.g., colonialism, British-American relationships, and Zionism.

520. Brogan, C. *Suez. What Was Right?* London: Coram, 1957.

521. Calvocoressi, Peter (editor, amongst others). *Suez: Ten Years after—Broadcasts from the BBC Third Programme.* New York: Pantheon Books, 1967. 160.

Broadcasts from the BBC Third Programme that give a fairly authentic background to the Suez War. It includes interviews with Nasser, Ben Gurion and many other participants in the 1956 conflict.

522. Cansacchi, G. "I termini giuridici e politici della controversia di Suez." (The Legal and Political Terms of the Suez Question). *Oriente Moderno*, February 1957.

523. Castaneda, J. "Certain Legal Consequences of the Suez Crisis." *Revue Égyptienne de Droit International*, 19, 1963: 1–15.

524. Charles-Roux, F. "Ce qui disparait d'Égypte avec la Compagnie Universelle du Canal Maritime de Suez" (What Egypt Loses with the Universal Company of the Suez Maritime Canal). *Revue des Travaux de l'Académie des Sciences Morales et Politiques*, July 1st 1957.

525. Charles-Roux, F. "Ce que la France perd avec le canal de Suez" (What France Loses with the Suez Canal). *La Nouvelle Revue Française d'Outre-Mer*, March 1957: 121–127.

526. Corbett, P. E. "Power and Law at Suez." *International Journal.* Canadian Institute of International Affairs, 12 (1), 1956–1957: 1–12.

527. De La Pradelle, R. "L'Égypte a-t-elle violé le droit international en nationalisant la Compagnie Universelle du Canal Maritime de Suez?" (Has Egypt Violated International Law in Nationalising the Suez Canal Company?). *Internationales Recht und Diplomatice* (International Law and Diplomacy), 1958: 20–27.

528. Dessouki, Sami H. *Suez Canal: Changing World 1956–2000.* London: Heinemann, 1982. 148.

A study of the investment into the Canal and of its implications for the future of Egypt and the rest of the world.

529. Dinitz, S. "The Legal Aspects of the Egyptian Blockade of the Suez Canal." *Georgetown Law Journal*, 45, 1956–1957: 169–199.

530. Eagleton, C. "The United Nations and the Suez Crisis." *Tensions in the Middle East*, editor: Thayer, P. W. Baltimore: Johns Hopkins University Press, 1958: 273–296.

531. Feis, H. "Suez Scenario: A Lamentable Tale." *Foreign Affairs*, 34 (4), 1960: 598–612.

532. Finch, G. A. "Post-mortem on the Suez Debacle." *American Journal of International Law*, 51, 1957: 376–380.

533. Finer, Herman. *Dulles over Suez: The Theory and Practice of His Diplomacy.* London: Heinemann, 1964. 538.

Although mainly aimed at students of Dulles, this work gives interesting insights into the United States diplomacy behind Suez.

534. Fitzsimons, M. A. "The Suez Crisis and the Containment Policy." *Review of Politics*, volume 19, October 1957: 419–45.

Analysis of the Eisenhower Doctrine and its implications for Soviet policy in the Arab World after Suez.

535. Flandin, P. E. "L'Affaire de Suez" (The Suez Affair). *Revue des Deux Mondes*, November 1956.

536. Flether, M. E. *Suez and Britain: An Historical Study.* Ph.D. the University of Wisconsin, 1957.

537. Foot, Michael and Jones, Mervyn. *Guilty Men, 1957*. London: Victor Gollancz Ltd., 1957. 264.

This is a severely critical study of Suez and its implications in the light of Britain's perceived guilt.

538. Friedmann, W. and Collins, L. A. "The Suez Canal Crisis of 1956." *International Law and Political Crisis*. Editors: Scheinman, L. and Wilkinson, D. Boston: Little Brown, 1968. 273.

539. Gamal, M. B. "Israel and the Suez Canal: A New Approach." *Egyptian Review of International Law*, 1961: 103–130.

540. Generales, M. D. "Suez—National Sovereignty and International Waterways." *Western Political Quarterly*, 10, 1957: 453–454.

541. Ghobashy, O. Z. "Egypt's Attitude towards International Law as Expressed in the U.N.—the Egyptian-Israeli Dispute on the Freedom of Navigation in the Suez Canal." *Revue Égyptienne de Droit International*, 11, 1955: 121–131.

542. Ghobashy, O. Z. "Israel and the Suez Canal." *Egyptian Economic and Political Review*, 4, 1960: 9–13.

543. G. L. "Suez and Its Consequences: The Israeli View." *World Today*, 13 (4), 1957: 152–161.

544. James, Robert Rhodes. "Anthony Eden and the Suez Crisis." *History Today*, volume 36, November 1986, 8+.

545. Jewish Agency. "Eilat instead of Suez Route." *Jewish Agency's Digest of Press and Events*, 10 (17), Haifa, 1956.

546. Kedourie, Elie. "It Started at Suez." *New Republic*, volume 186, May 26 1982: 19+.

547. Lacoste, R. "La crise de Suez et le déclin de l'Europe" (The Suez Crisis and the Decline of Europe). *Revue Générale belge*, January 1957.

548. Lavergne, B. "L'affaire de Suez ou la dernière infidélité des États-Unis. La fin du Pacte Atlantique" (The Suez Affair or the Last U.S. Betrayal. The End of the Atlantic Pact). *L'Année Politique et Économique*, 29 (132), 1956: 350–386.

549. Lauterpacht, E. (editor). *The Suez Canal Settlement: a selection of documents relating to the settlement of the Suez Canal dispute, the*

clearance of the Suez Canal and the settlement of disputes between the United Kingdom, France and the United Arab Republic, October 1956—March 1959. Published under the auspices of the British Institute of International and Comparative Law. London: Stevens, 1960. 82.

550. Louis, William Roger and Owen, Roger. *Suez 1956: The Crisis and Its Consequences.* Oxford: The Clarendon Press, 1989. 428.

A collection of papers written by various persons some of whom were involved in the Suez War. The papers seek to put Suez in perspective thirty years later showing its effect—or lack of it—on local and world politics.

551. Marcos, S. A. "Effect of the Aswan High Dam on the Current Régime in the Suez Canal." *Nature*, 214, 1967: 901–902.

552. Milliot, L. "La crise égyptiénne de Suez" (The Egyptian Suez Crisis). *Comptes Rendus, Académie de Sciences Coloniales*, November 1956.

553. National Bank of Egypt. "The Suez Canal—Ten Years of Egyptian Management." *Economic Bulletin*, 19 (3), 1966: 253–261.

554. Nutting, A. *I Saw for Myself: The Aftermath of Suez.* London: Hollis and Carter, 1958.

555. Robertson, Terence. *Crisis: The Inside Story of the Suez Conspiracy.* London: Hutchinson, 1965. 339. New York: Atheneum, 1965. 349.

A narrative of the political intrigue and the tripartite conspiracy that led to the 1956 war. Largely a British analysis of Suez. Although no Egyptians were consulted in the process of research and writing, the book manages to steer a comparatively neutral course.

556. Rowie, Robert R. *International Crises and the Role of Law: Suez 1956.* New York; London: Oxford University Press, 1974. 148.

The author analyses the part played by international law in the Suez crisis showing how participants' actions were governed by such law.

557. Schonfield, Hugh J. *The Suez Canal in Peace and War, 1869–1969.* London: Mitchell, Vellentine; Coral Gables, Florida: University of Miami Press, 1969. 214.

An attempt to reconcile Egypt's sovereignty over the Canal and the world's right to use it. The book gives a history of the Canal from Lesseps to 1967.

558. Slovenko, R. "Nationalization and Nasser." *International Law and the Middle East Crisis.* New Orleans: Tulane University Press, 1957: 79–93.

559. United Nations. "The Impact of the Suez Crisis." *Economic Survey of Europe in 1956,* Department of Economic and Social Affairs, Geneva, iii, 1957: 33–37.

560. United Nations. "Preliminary Review of the Economic Impact of the Suez Canal Crisis on the Middle East." *Economic Developments in the Middle East 1955–1956: Supplement to World Economic Survey 1956,* Department of Economic and Social Affairs, New York, 1957: 99–112.

561. Wouters, H. E. "The Suez Canal Crisis and Its Consequences." *Capital* (Supplement) December 1956.

See also:

Blake, G. H. and Swearingen, W. D. (editors). *The Suez Canal: A Commemorative Bibliography* 1975. (no. 813).

VIII. Non-Alignment

Non-alignment was a pivotal anchor point of Nasser's professed foreign policy. Two points must be borne in mind in considering it: Firstly Nasser's genuine idealism caused him to join the Non-aligned movement regardless of its inherent political weakness and its consequence to Egypt's position. Secondly, being non-aligned was regarded by the superpowers with great suspicion. Both the Americans and the Russians regarded Non-alignment, or Neutralism as some called it, as a serious threat to their hegemony. With such opposing tensions at work, Non-alignment was soon to become an ideology with no basis in political practice.

562. Burton, J. W. (editor). *Nonalignment*. London: Deutsch, 1966.

563. Nash, Marguerite Bou-Raad. *National Interest and Neutralism in Nasser's Foreign Policy: Three Case Studies*. Ph.D. The University of North Carolina at Chapel Hill, 1977. 655. (Volume 39/10–A of *Dissertation Abstracts International*, page 455).

564. Rubinstein, Alvin Z. "Politics in Flux." *Problems of Communism* 17, number 2, March-April 1968: 31–40.

Yugoslavia's Communist Party reforms of the 1960s and Non-alignment.

565. Rubinstein, Alvin Z. *Yugoslavia and the Nonaligned World*. Princeton, New Jersey: Princeton University Press, 1969. 353.

566. Stojkovic, Momir M. *Tito, Nehru, Naser: nastanak i razvoj politike i pokreta nesvrstanosti* (The Creation and Development of the Policy of the Nonaligned Movement). Belgrade: R J izdavacka. delatnost u Beogradu, 1983. 392.

An examination of the relationship between the main leaders of Nonalignment. English readers may wish to refer to Heikal's *The Cairo Documents* for a similar treatment of the subject (see number 330 above).

567. Tito, Josip Broz. "President Tito and Non-Alignment." *Socialist Thought and Practice 19*, number 9, September 1979: 3–31.

Extracts from speeches on Non-alignment.

568. Tito, Josip Broz. *Non-Alignment: The Conscience and Future of Mankind.* Belgrade: Socialist Thought and Practice, 1980. 170.

569. Tito, Josip Broz. "Non-alignment: Universal Movement for Peace." *Socialist Thought and Practice*, number 12, October-December 1963: 5–17.

Speeches on Non-alignment.

570. Tito, Josip Broz. "The Historical Responsibility of the Movement of Non-Alignment." *Socialist Thought and Practice*, number 10, October 1979: 3–14.

Speeches on Non-alignment.

571. Tito, Josip Broz. *Belgrade Conference: The Speeches of President Josip Broz Tito.* Belgrade: Jugoslavija, 1961. 49.

On Non-alignment.

572. *U.S. News and World Report.* "Nehru and Nasser." Volume 46, April 13 1959: 70+.

See also:

Heikal, Mohamed. *Nasser: The Cairo Documents.* (no. 330).

IX. Pan-Arabism

The Arab cold war, as it came to be known, had a plethora of participants. It is not possible to cover such a huge and complex subject adequately within the present limits. Sources given below are those specifically relevant to Nasser's direct involvement in Pan-Arab affairs. Many publications listed have comprehensive bibliographies offering the possibility of further study.

A. Domestic

573. Abdalla, Ahmed. *The Student Movement and National Politics in Egypt, 1923–1973*. London: Al Saqi Books (distributor: Zed Books), 1985. 281.

A useful book covering student activities before and during Nasser's leadership.

574. Abdel-Fadil, Mahmoud. *The Political Economy of Nasserism: A Study in Employment and Income Distribution Policies in Urban Egypt, 1952–72*. Cambridge: Cambridge University Press, 1980. 140.

Despite its specialised jargon, a very readable book that analyses Nasserist political economy. Chapter 7 on "The Limits of Nasserism" is well argued and interesting. Well tabulated stastistics give an overview of Nasser's economic performance.

575. Abdel-Malek, Anouar. *Égypte, Société Militaire*. Paris: Édition du Seuil, 1962. 379. Available in English as: *Egypt: Military Society:*

The Army Régime, the Left, and Social Change under Nasser. New York: Random House, 1968. 458.

A Marxist analysis of Nasser's Egypt by an Egyptian scholar who was actively opposed to Nasser's policies.

576. Ahmed, J. H. *The Intellectual Origins of Egyptian Nationalism.* Oxford: Oxford University Press, 1960.

Published under the auspices of the Royal Institute of International Affairs.

577. Ansari, Hamid N. "The Islamic Militants in Egyptian Politics." *International Journal of Middle East Studies*, volume 16, number 1, March 1985: 123–44.

Showing how urbanization produced alienation within certain sections of the community thus allowing for an expansion of Islamic fundamentalism in Egypt.

578. Ansari, Hamid N. "Sectarian Conflict in Egypt and the Political Expediency of Religion." *Middle East Journal*, volume 38, number 3, Summer 1984: 397–418.

Shows how Sadat's attempts to move away from the Nasserist formula of mass political mobilization backfired in causing a resurgence of Islamic militancy in Egypt.

579. Beattie, Kirk James. *Egypt: The Struggle for Hegemony, 1952–1981.* Two volumes. The University of Michigan, 1985. 428. (Volume 46/04-A of *Dissertation Abstracts International*, page 1072).

A study of Nasser's hegemony over Egypt in a failed attempt to fulfill socio-economic development objectives. The failure is seen as caused by opposition and extra-régime influences.

580. Beinin, Joel. "The Communist Movement and Nationalist Political Discourse in Nasirist Egypt." *Middle East Journal*, volume 41, issue 4, Autumn 1987: 568–584.

581. Berindranath, Dewan. *Nasser: The Man and the Miracle.* New Delhi: Afro-Asian Publications, 1966. 111.

An analysis of Nasser as a charismatic leader.

582. Berque, Jacques. *L'Égypte: Imperialisme et Révolution.* Paris: Gallimard, 1967. 746.

With decolonization as its central theme; this work deals with a broad social view of Egyptian history.

583. Carre, Olivier. "The Impact of the Egyptian Muslim Brotherhood's Political Islam since the 1950s." *Islam, Nationalism and Radicalism in Egypt and the Sudan.* Edited by Warburg, Gabriel R. and Kupferschmidt, Uri M. New York: Praeger, 1983. 262.

Showing how the Muslim Brotherhood ideology affected Nasser's politics.

584. Childers, Erskine and McKenzie, Robert. "Gamal Abdel Nasser." *Listener*, May 19th 1966: 707+.

An interview with Nasser.

585. Childers, Erskine B. "Nasser." *Spectator*, May 4th 1962: 612+.

586. Childers, Erskine. "Nasser's Front Door." *Guardian*, April 27th 1966: 10+.

587. Gersh, Gabriel. "Nasser's Brand of Socialism." *Christian Century*, volume 81, July 29th 1964: 962+.

588. Gershoni, Israel. *The Emergence of Pan-Arabism in Egypt.* Tel Aviv, Israel: Shiloah Centre for Middle Eastern and African Studies, Tel Aviv University, 1981. 142.

A study of the emergence of Pan-Arabism in Egypt with the conclusion that the period covering 1936–1940 was a crucial one in the development of Pan-Arab ideology.

589. Holden, David. "Nasser as a One-man Democracy: Régime's Need of Legal Basis." *Guardian*, January 2nd 1963: 8+.

590. Jankowski, James P. "Nationalism in Twentieth-century Egypt." *The Middle East Reader*, Editor: Curtis, Michael. New Brunswick, New Jersey; Oxford: Transaction Books, 1986. 193–204.

A readable condensed view of Egyptian nationalism from the 1850s to the advent of Nasser.

591. El-Kosheri Mahfouz, Afaf. *Socialisme et pouvoir en Égypte* (Socialism and Power in Egypt). Paris: Bibliothèque constitutionelle et science politique, volume 44, 1972. 292.

592. Lacouture, Jean and Lacouture, Simone. *L'Égypte en Mouvement.* Paris: Editions du Seuil, 1956. 480. An expanded English translation is available: *Egypt in Transition.* New York: Criterion Books, 1958. 532. London: Methuen, 1958.

The work deals with Egypt's difficulties in solving many of its major problems. It also has sections on the Free Officers, on Nasser, on Suez and on Egypt's agrarian and economic development plans.

593. *Land Reform Law: Full Text.* Cairo: Press Department, 1955. 31.

Nasser's land reform limiting ownership to 200 acres.

594. Mabro, Robert. *The Egyptian Economy 1952–1972.* Oxford: Clarendon Press.

An economic appraisal of Nasser's régime with specific references to the general nature of economic development.

595. Mabro, Robert and Radwan, Samir. *The Industrialization of Egypt 1939–1973: Policy and Performance.* Oxford: Clarendon Press, 1976. 276.

596. Marsot, Afaf Lutfi al-Sayyid. "Religion or Opposition? Urban Protest Movements in Egypt." *International Journal of Middle East Studies*, volume 16, number 4, November 1984: 541–52.

597. Mayfield, James B. *Rural Politics in Nasser's Egypt: A Quest for Legitimacy.* Austin, Texas: University of Texas Press, 1971. 270.

Under Nasser, the Egyptian village was politically run by centrally appointed administrators, the old village council and the local branch of the A.S.U. (Arab Socialist Union). This book shows the extent of the success or failure of the three interlocking forces.

598. O'Brien, Patrick. *The Revolution in Egypt's Economic System: From Private Enterprise to Socialism, 1952–1965.* New York: Oxford University Press (for the Royal Institute of International Affairs), 1966. 354.

A description of the institutional changes introduced by Nasser in order to re-organise the Egyptian economy. O'Brien shows a continuity in Egypt's economy as state controlled rather than ideologically socialist.

599. Powell, Ivor. *Disillusion by the Nile: What Nasser Has Done to Egypt.* London: Solstice Productions, 1967. 137.

600. Rejwan, Nissim. *Nasserite Ideology: Its Exponents and Critics.* New York: John Wiley; Jerusalem: Israel Universities Press, 1974. 271.

An analysis of Nasser's ideology including the script of The Charter on pages 192–265.

601. Riad, Hassan. *L'Égypte Nasserienne* (Nasser's Egypt). Paris: Édition de Minuit, 1964. 249.

An Egyptian Marxist's view of Nasser's Egypt.

602. Shinnawi, Fahmi. *al-Nasiriyah wathaniyah siyasiyah* (Nasserist National Politics). Cairo: Kitab al-Mukhtar, 1989. 197.

603. Sparrow, Gerald. *The Sphinx Awakes.* London: Robert Hale Ltd., 1956. 217.

A history of Nasser's Egypt. Its appendices include the Arab League Charter and Nasser's political Testament—the latter is worth reading for a flavour of Nasser's vision.

See also:

El-Ashram, Mohamed Abdel-Halim. *Nasser's Ideology and Organization: A Modernizing Experiment in Egypt, 1952–1970.* (no. 795).

Nasser, Gamal A. *Our People's Meeting with Destiny.* (no. 320).

Nasser, Gamal A. *Speeches on the Occasion of the Thirteenth Anniversary of the Revolution, July 1965.* (no. 324).

Nasir, Shawqi Abd al-. *Thawrat Abd al-Nasir.* (no. 325).

B. Foreign

604. Abbas, Jabir Ali. *Points of Departure in Egypt's Foreign Policy: The Essence of Nasser's Power.* Ph.D. Indiana University, 1969. 398. (Volume 32/10–A of *Dissertation Abstracts International*, page 5846).

605. Abbas, Mekki. *The Sudan Question.* New York: Praeger, 1952. 201.

A work by a Sudanese that explores the central role of the Sudan in Anglo-Egyptian relations.

606. Abdul Alim, A. K. M. "A Study of Nasser's Leadership in the Arab World." *Dacca University Studies*, Bangladesh, part Q (20), 1972: 23–29.

Assesses the strengths and weaknesses of Nasser's leadership with emphasis on his failure to unite the Arab world.

607. Abu Izzeddin, Nejla M. *Nasser of the Arabs: An Arab Assessment.* London: Third World Centre for Research and Publishing, 1981. 467. Beirut: Imprimerie Catholique, 1981. 467.

An Arab analysis of Nasser and his policies. Shows Nasser as an Arab leader whose foreign policy was closely related to the necessities of his domestic affairs.

608. Agwami, M. S. (editor). *The Lebanese Crisis: A Documentary Study.* Bombay: Asia Publishing House, 1965.

609. Ajami, Fouad. "On Nasser and His Legacy." *Journal of Peace Research* (Norway), 11 (1), 1974: 41-49.

A review of Heikal's *The Cairo Documents*. Nasser is seen as a rebel in search of Egypt's dignity.

610. Badeeb, Saeed M. *The Saudi-Egyptian Conflict over North Yemen, 1962–1970.* Boulder, Colorado: Westview Press; Washington, D.C.: American Arab Affairs Council, 1986. 148.

An analysis of the Yemeni coup of 1962 which led to a war between the Republicans (supported by Egypt) and the Monarchists (supported by Saudi Arabia).

611. Campobasso, Carina. *Conflict within the Context of Two Personalized Régimes: Nasser and Bourguiba: A Political Comparison.* Geneva: Institut universitaire de hautes études internationales, 1984. 106.

Nasser and Bourguiba had a confrontation over the latter's advice of an Arab settlement with Israel. It may be said that Bourguiba articulated what Nasser secretly believed in although his timing was inopportune. It is ironic that Nasser's immediate successor signed a peace treaty with Israel which delivered the very peace that Bourguiba had referred to earlier.

612. Childers, Erskine. "British Bumbling the Despair of Arab Socialists." *Guardian*, April 28th 1966: 14+.

613. Crane, P. H. "Nasser and Kassem: a Study in Acrimonious Coexistence." *The Reporter*, volume 20, June 25th 1959: 20+.

Kassem was the Iraqi leader who ousted the Iraqi Royal Family. After a friendly start he and Nasser became bitter enemies.

614. Cremeans, Charles D. *The Arabs and the World: Nasser's Arab Nationalist Policy*. New York; London: Praeger for the Council on Foreign Relations. 1963. 324.

A detailed study of Nasser's first few years including the ill fated union with Syria and much of his foreign policies especially in Africa and Asia. Also discussed is the optimism that characterized the lapsed Kennedy-Nasser interlude. Cremeans was on diplomatic assignment in Egypt in 1955 when he met Nasser and many others.

615. Dawisha, A. I. *Egypt in the Arab World: the Elements of Foreign Policy*. London: Macmillan; New York: Wiley, 1976. 234.

The first part includes an analysis of Egypt's Arab policy between 1952 and 1970.

616. Dawisha, A. I. "Intervention in the Yemen: An Analysis of Egyptian Perceptions and Policies." *Middle East Journal*, volume 29, number 1, Winter 1975: 47–63.

617. Dawisha, A. I. "Perceptions, Decisions and Consequences in Foreign Policy: The Egyptian Intervention in the Yemen." *Political Studies* (Great Britain), 25 (2), 1977: 201-226.

618. Dib, Mohamed F. *Abdel Nasser et la révolution algerienne* (Nasser and the Algerian Revolution). Paris: L'Harmattan, 1985. 443.

Nasser became heavily involved in the Algerian revolution with serious repercussions in relations with France.

619. Fallatah, Mohammed A. S. *The Emergence of Pan-Arabism and Its Impact on Egyptian Foreign Policy: 1945–1981*. Ph.D. University of Idaho, 1986. 347. (Volume 47/10–A of *Dissertation Abstracts International*, page 3864).

An investigation of how the Pan-Arab ideal influenced Egyptian foreign policy making it less pragmatic under Nasser. The utopian dream is seen as destructive of Egypt's national interests.

620. Fayiq, Muhammad Muhammad. *Abd al-Nasir wa-al-thawrah al-Afriqiyah* (Nasser and the African Revolution). Cairo: Dar al-Mustaqbal al-Arabi, 1982. 198.

621. Flinn, Peter. "President Nasser and the Arab World." *Listener*, March 25th 1965: 437+.

622. Gilead, Baruch. "Turkish-Egyptian Relations 1952–1957." *Middle Eastern Affairs*, volume 10, November 1959: 356–66.

Analyses the rivalry between Egypt and Turkey for the position of leadership in the Middle East.

623. Gott, Richard. "The Break-up of the United Arab Republic, Its Effect on Inter-Arab Relations, 1961-2." *Survey of International Affairs, 1962*. Edited by Watt, D. C. London; New York: Oxford University Press, 1970: 465–81.

Nasser's alienation of the main currents of Syrian political life is seen as the major reason for the break-up of the U.A.R.

624. Hanna, Sami A. and Gardner, George H. *Arab Socialism: A Documentary Survey*. Salt Lake City, Utah: University of Utah Press, 1969. 418.

A vast amount of basic source material from the Arab world was consulted in writing this work on socialism in Arab society.

625. Harris, Christina Phelps. *Nationalism and Revolution in Egypt*. The Hague, 1966.

626. Hasour, Tawfiq Yousef. *The Arab League in Egyptian Foreign Policy under Gamal Abdel-Nasser: A Study of International Regional Organization in the Foreign Policy of Small States*. Ph.D. University of Virginia, 1979. 361. (Volume 40/09–A of Dissertation Abstracts International, page 5173).

627. Hasour, Tawfiq Y. *The Struggle for the Arab World: Egypt's Nasser and the Arab League*. London (Boston: KPI) distributed by Routledge and Kegan Paul, 1985. 228.

Arab League dealings have often bemused, confused and amused the Western observer. This work will go some way towards explaining some of these dealings. Nasser's use of the Arab League to promote his own policies is also explored.

628. Holden, David. "President Nasser's Predicament." *Guardian*, January 14th 1964: 8+.

629. Horton, Philip. "Our Yemen Policy: Pursuit of a Mirage." *The Reporter*, volume 29, October 24th 1963: 28+.

On the United States' handling of Nasser's war in the Yemen.

630. Hurewitz, J. C. *Middle East Politics: The Military Dimension*. New York: Praeger (for the Council on Foreign Relations), 1969. 553.

A study of military politics in eighteen states from Morocco to Afghanistan.

631. Hussein, King of Jordan. *Uneasy Lies the Head*. London: Heinemann: 1962. A very readable work which sheds light on Jordanian-Egyptian relations and other relevant events.

632. Ismael, Tareq Y. *The Arab Left*. Syracuse, New York: Syracuse University Press, 1976. 204.

Including sections on Nasserism, Arab Nationalism, and Egyptian socialism.

633. Ismael, Tareq Y. *The U.A.R. in Africa*. Evanston: Northwestern University Press, 1971. 258.

An analysis of Egypt's African and other policies under Nasser with specific reference to the Sudan and the Congo.

634. Karanjia, Rustom Khurshedji. *The Arab Dawn*. Bombay: Jaico Publishing House, 1958. 360.

The work also contains a foreword by Nasser.

635. Kerr, Malcom H. *The Arab Cold War: Gamal Abd al-Nasir and His Rivals 1958–1970*. London: Oxford University Press (for the Royal Institute of International Affairs), 1971. 166.

An update of a previously published work (see number 636 below). In the light of differing Arab ideologies and aspirations, Nasser's attempt to manipulate the other Arab states did not always meet with success.

636. Kerr, Malcolm. *The Arab Cold War, 1958–1964: A Study of Ideology in Politics*. New York: Oxford University Press (for the Royal Institute of International Affairs), 1965. 139.

An interpretative essay with emphasis on Egypt's foreign policy and the role of Arab Nationalism. The work was later updated (see number 635 above).

637. King, Gillian. *Documents on International Affairs, 1958*. London: Oxford University Press, 1962. 605.

Including the proclamation of the United Arab Republic and the Constitution of the United Arab States (i.e., United Arab Republic and Yemen.)

638. Laqueur, Walter Z. *Communism and Nationalism in the Middle East*. New York: Praeger, 1956. 362.

A work which contains a great deal on Arab Communist parties and Middle East Politics in the mid-fifties.

639. Laqueur, Walter Z. "Nasser and the Iraqi Communists." *Commentary*, volume 27, February 1959: 101+.

640. Legum, Colin. *Pan Africanism*. London: Pall Mall, 1962.

641. Lerner, Daniel. *The Passing of Traditional Society: Modernizing the Middle East*. Glencoe: Free Press, 1958. 466.

Egypt is one of the six Middle Eastern countries studied through interviews with some three hundred individuals in each country. A good work to read in order to gain an insight into the Egyptian's individual and social psychology. Since the approach used is that of a behavioral scientist, there are some interesting insights to be gained.

642. Little, Tom. *Modern Egypt*. London: Ernest Benn, 1967. 300.

An expansive update of Little's earlier work on Egypt (see number 396 above) to include the early sixties and the Six Day War.

643. Malone, Joseph J. "A Middle East Power, Egypt, Mainspring of Arab Power." *Emerging Powers, Defense and Security in the Third World*. Edited by Jones, Rodney W. and Hildreth, Steven A. New York: Praeger, in co-operation with the Center for Strategic and International Studies, Georgetown University, 1986: 223–66.

Egypt's role as the major regional power is analysed. Its power is based on its Islamic, cultural and intellectual leadership.

644. Mansfield, Peter. "Nasser's Yemen Headache." *Sunday Times*, February 5th 1967: 10+.

645. Maqalih, Abdel Aziz. *Abd al-Nasir wa-al-Yaman: fusul min tarikh al-thawrah al-Yamaniyah* (Nasser and the Yemen: A Chapter of the Yemeni Revolution). Beirut: Dar al-Hadathah, 1983. 152.

646. Mazrui, Ali A. "Africa and the Egyptian's Four Circles." *African Affairs*, April 1964: 129+.

647. Muzikar, Josef. "Arab Nationalism and Islam." *Archiv Orientalni* (Czechoslovakia), 43 (4), 1975: 302–323.

On Nasser's Arab socialism.

648. Nuseibeh, Hazem Zaki. *The Ideas of Arab Nationalism.* New York: 1956.

649. Palmer, Monte. "The United Arab Republic: Assessment of Its Failure." *Middle East Journal*, volume 20, number 1, Winter 1966: 50–67.

Syrian discontent is seen as the major factor in the dissolution of the United Arab Republic.

650. Qubain, Fahim I. *Crisis in Lebanon.* Washington, D.C.: Middle East Institute, 1961.

A useful backdrop to Nasser's involvement in the 1958 Lebanese civil war.

651. Rahmy, Ali Abdel Rahman. *The Egyptian Policy in the Arab World. Intervention in Yemen, 1962–1967: Case Study.* Washington, D.C.: University Press of America, 1983. 391.

652. Raouf, Wafik. *Nouveau regard sur le nationalisme arabe: Ba'th et Nasserisme* (A New Look at Arab Nationalism: Ba'thism and Nasserism). Paris: Collections Racines du present, 1984. 380.

653. Seale, Patrick. "The Break-up of the United Arab Republic." *World Today*, volume 17, number 11, November 1961: 471-9.

Throws an insight into Nasser's reaction to the Syrian secession from the United Arab Republic.

654. Schmidt, Dana Adams. *Yemen: The Unknown War.* London: Bodley Head, 1968.

See also:

Nasser, Gamal A. *On the Road to African Unity; the Fourth Summit Conference, November 5, 1966.* (no. 319).

Nasser, Gamal A. *President Gamal Abdel Nasser on Consolidation of the Cause of World Peace.* (no. 321).

Supreme Council for Islamic Affairs. *The Islamic Pact, an Obvious Trick.* (no. 317).

X. The Battle for Palestine

An attempt has been made to give as many representative viewpoints as possible. Consequently some of the Arab or Palestinian sources will be less easy to find. Specialist bookshops or major libraries stock the majority of the following titles.

A. Arab-Israeli Conflict

655. Abu-Lughod, Ibrahim. *The Arab-Israeli Confrontation of June 19-67: An Arab Perspective.* Evanston, Ill.: Northwestern University Press, 1970.

A collection of essays critical of Western attitudes to the 1967 war, including analyses of the media coverage, the United Nations pronouncements, etc.

656. Bailey, Sydney D. *Four Arab-Israeli Wars and the Peace Process.* London: Macmillan, 1982 (reprinted 1990). 522.

A study of the four Arab-Israeli wars of 48, 56, 67, and 73 with emphasis on each of the post-war mediation attempts. The author challenges the perceived wisdom that face-to-face encounters between adversaries with a similar power base are best.

657. Burns, Eedson Louis Millard. *Between Arab and Israeli.* New York: Obolensky, 1963. 336.

General Burns writes from first hand experience as a United Nations Force Commander in the mid-fifties. The work includes a section on the Israeli attack on Egypt during the Suez crisis of 1956.

658. Churchill, Winston and Randolph. *The Six-Day War*. London: Heinemann, 1967.

An account of the June 1967 war with a brief historical background. An appendix discusses the B.B.C.'s coverage of the war.

659. Dupuy, Trevor N. *Elusive Victory: The Arab-Israeli Wars, 1957–1974*. London: Macdonald & Jane's, 1978. 633.

A military history of the Arab-Israeli conflicts.

660. Gabbay, Rony E. *A Political Study of the Arab-Jewish Conflict: The Arab Refugee Problem (A Case Study)*. Geneva: Droz, 1959. 611.

A work that deals with the Palestinian refugee problem from every aspect.

661. Hirst, David. *The Gun and the Olive Branch: The Roots of Violence in the Middle East*. New York: Harcourt Brace Jovanovich, 1977.

662. Hussein, King of Jordan. *My "War" with Israel*. New York: 1969.

A readable work on Jordan's involvement in the 1967 war.

663. Khouri, Fred J. *The Arab-Israeli Dilemma*. Syracuse: Syracuse University Press, 1968. 436.

This is a comprehensive and well-documented study of the Arab-Israeli conflict. An appendix includes some relevant documents.

664. Laqueur, Walter. *The Road to War 1967: The Origins of the Arab-Israel Conflict*. London: Weidenfeld & Nicolson, 1968. 352.

Covering the Arab-Israeli wars up to the Six-Day War in 1967. Appendices include important documents and speeches relating to the 1967 war.

665. O'Ballance, Edgar. *The Electronic War in the Middle East 1968–70*. London: Faber & Faber; Hamden, Connecticut: Archon Books, 1974. 148.

On the war of attrition between Israel and Egypt with references to the role played by the superpowers.

666. O'Ballance, Edgar. *The Third Arab-Israeli War*. London: Faber & Faber, 1972. 279.

An account of the 1967 war.

667. Ovendale, Ritchie. *The Origins of the Arab-Israeli Wars.* London and New York: Longman, 1984. 232.

668. Rikhye, Indar Jit. *The Sinai Blunder.* London: Cass, 1980.

United Nations analysis of mistakes that helped spark off the 1967 war.

669. Rodinson, Maxime. *Israel and the Arabs.* London: Penguin, 1968. 239.

Rodinson is a French Marxist sociologist of Jewish origins. An analysis of the Arab-Israeli conflict tracing the development of Zionism and the changing face of Pan-Arabism. It is mildly critical of Western attitudes as oversimplistic and as lacking an understanding of Arab politics.

670. Safran, Nadav. *From War to War: The Arab-Israeli Confrontation, 1948–1967.* New York: Pegasus, 1969. 464.

An analysis of the Arab-Israeli conflicts within the context of the cold war and inter-Arab relations. The work also has a significant detailed military analysis of the conflict.

671. Sterling, Claire. "Never-ended War of the Middle East." *The Reporter,* volume 29, July 18th 1963: 24+.

672. U.S. News and World Report. "The Cost of Self-deception." Volume 102, June 8th 1987:36+.

On how Egypt and Jordan lost the Six-Day War in 1967.

673. Yizhar, Michael. "Israel and the Eisenhower Doctrine." *Wiener Library Bulletin,* 28:33/34, 1975: 58–64.

See also:

Nasser, Gamal A. and Kennedy, John F. *Lil-haqiqah wa-al-tarikh, al mushkilah al Filastiniyah. (no. 314).*

Nasser, Gamal Abdel. "Memoirs of the First Palestine War." (no. 311).

B. Israel

674. Bar-Zohar, Michael. *Ben-Gurion: A Biography.* Translated by Peretz Kidron. New York: Delacorte, 1978.

675. Ben-Gurion, David. *Negotiations with Nasser*. Jerusalem: Israel Information Centre, 1973. 64.

676. Dayan, Moshe. *Moshe Dayan: Story of My Life*. New York: Morrow. London: Weidenfeld and Nicolson, 1976. 530.

Despite its title this work contains very little on Dayan's early life. Its emphasis is on the 1948, 1956, 1967 and 1973 Arab-Israeli wars.

677. Draper, Theodore. *Israel and World Politics: Roots of the Third Arab-Israeli War*. New York: Viking, 1968.

Includes substantial documents on the war and the pre-war events of May 1967.

678. Eban, Abba. *Abba Eban: An Autobiography*. New York: Random House, 1977.

Abba Eban's memoirs from his early life to his service as Israel's ambassador to the United States and its minister of foreign affairs.

679. Eban, A. S. "The Story of a Blockade." *Voice of Israel*, London: Faber, 1958.

680. Howard, Michael and Hunter, Robert. *Israel and the Arab World: The Crisis of 1967*. Adelphi Paper number 41. London: International Institute for Strategic Studies. 1967.

A short overview of the war giving general background and immediate origins.

681. Pearlman, Moshe. *Ben-Gurion Looks Back in Talks with Moshe Pearlman*. New York: Simon and Schuster, 1965.

682. Perlmutter, Amos. *Military and Politics in Israel: Nation-Building and Role Expansion*. New York: Praeger, 1969. 161.

683. Rodinson, Maxime. *Israel: A Colonial-Settler State?* New York: Monad Press, 1973. 120.

A documented analysis of the formation of Israel.

684. Sykes, Christopher. *Cross Roads to Israel*. Cleveland: World, 1965. 404.

A Zionist view of the history of Palestine partly critical of Israel's propaganda machine and alleged unrealized ideals. The work covers the early history of Zionism up to the creation of Israel on 15th May, 1948.

See also:

Laqueur, Walter (editor). *The Israeli-Arab Reader*. (no. 378).

Shipler, David K. *Arab and Jew: Wounded Spirits in a Promised Land*. (no. 379).

C. Palestine

685. Glubb, Sir John Bagot. *A Soldier with the Arabs*. New York: Harper, 1958. 458.

John Glubb was in command of the Jordanian Arab Legion. His analysis is sympathetic to Jordan and critical of Britain. The 1948–49 Arab-Israeli war receives some detailed treatment.

686. Hadawi, Sami. *Bitter Harvest: Palestine between 1914–1967*. New York: The New World Press, 1967. 355.

A well documented history of the Arab-Israeli conflict.

687. Hall, Donna Jean. *The Political Agenda of the Palestine Liberation Organisation*. M.A. CBN University, 1989. 83. (Volume 28/01 of *Masters Abstracts*, page 60.)

A study purporting to show how the United Nations issued resolutions and created agencies designed to help the P.L.O.'s aim of destroying Israel and establishing a Palestinian state in its place.

688. Hurewitz, Jacob Coleman. *The Struggle for Palestine*. New York: Norton, 1950. 404.

One of the earlier works on the Arab-Israeli conflict giving a political history of the problem up to 1949.

689. Khalidi, Walid and Khadduri, Jill (editors). *Palestine and the Arab-Israeli Conflict: An Annotated Bibliography*. Beirut: Institute for Palestine Studies, 1974.

690. Polk, William Roe; Stamler, David M.; Asfour, Edmund. *Backdrop to Tragedy: The Struggle for Palestine*. Boston: Beacon Press, 1957. 399.

This is a work that delves into the emotional and psychological elements of the problem. It investigates the establishment of Israel, the Jews in Palestine, the Arabs in Palestine and the economic backdrop to the Palestinian tragedy.

691. Said, Edward W. *The Question of Palestine*. London: Routledge and Kegan Paul, 1980. 265.

An analysis of modern Palestinian nationhood. The author uses the techniques of literary criticism to highlight the reality of being Palestinians (as a nation of people) though homeless (as a state).

See also:

Jeffries, Joseph Mary Nagle. *Palestine: The Reality*. (no. 377).

D. Egypt

692. Ajami, Fouad. "The Resolution that Failed." *Nation*, volume 232, May 9th 1981: 569+.

Evaluation of Nasser and George Habbash, the latter being the founder of the Popular Front for the Liberation of Palestine guerrilla movement after the 1967 war.

693. Brand, Laurie. "Nasir's Egypt and the Reemergence of the Palestinian National Movement." *Journal of Palestine Studies*, 17, Winter 1988: 29–45.

Origins of the Palestinian community in Egypt with emphasis on women's, workers' and students' unions.

694. Cohen, Amnon and Baer, Gabriel. *Egypt and Palestine: A Millennium of Association (868–1948)*. New York: St. Martin's Press, 1984. 390.

A collection of studies covering the pre-Ottoman period, the Ottoman period and the 20th century.

695. Edmead, Frank. "Nasser, the Arab Leader Who Overreached Himself." *Guardian*, June 10th 1967: 7+.

696. *The Egyptian-Israeli Treaty: Text and Selected Documents*. Basic Documentary Series number 13. Beirut: Institute for Palestine Studies, 1979. 124.

697. Hurani, Faysal. *Abd al-Nasir wa-qadiyat Filastin: qira'ah li-afkarihi wa-mumarasatih* (Nasser and the Palestine Question: Theory and Practice). 'Akka: Dar al-Aswar, Mu'assasat al-Thaqafah al-Filastini-yah, 1987. 85.

An Arab analysis of Nasser and Palestine.

698. Jackson, Elmore. *Middle East Mission: The Story of a Major Bid for Peace in the Time of Nasser and Ben-Gurion.* New York; London: W. W. Norton, 1983. 124.

On Nasser's attempts to achieve a political settlement with Israel. After his failure to obtain arms from the U.S. Nasser tried his hand at a peace settlement with Israel in order not to have to turn to the U.S.S.R. for help.

699. Jankowski, James. "Egyptian Responses to the Palestine Problem in the Interwar Period." *International Journal of Middle East Studies*, volume 12, number 1, August 1980, 1–38.

Showing how the Palestine problem became a focus of Egyptian political awareness during Nasser's student years.

700. Mayer, Thomas. *Egypt and the Palestine Question, 1936–1945.* Berlin, GFR: Klaus Schwarz Verlag, 1983. 391.

Egypt became the focus for Arab Nationalism and a main defender of the Palestinian cause as this books describes in a well-documented way. An interesting analysis of Egypt's verbal support for the Arab League as opposed to the negligible progress made in practical terms.

701. Miller, Aaron David. "Egypt and the Palestinian Cause: Benefit and Burden." *The Arab States and the Palestine Question: between Ideology and Self-interest.* New York: Praeger Scientific, with the Centre for Strategic and International Studies, The Washington Papers, number 120, Georgetown University, Washington, D.C., 1986: 53–67.

Showing how, because of its geopolitical and historical background, Egypt was able to adopt a slightly more flexible and detached policy towards Palestine than Jordan or Syria.

702. Sachar, Howard M. *Egypt and Israel.* New York: Richard Marek Publishers, 1981. 384.

An account of Egyptian-Israeli relations from 1948 to 1979 when the peace treaty was signed.

703. Schueftan, Dan. "Nasser's 1967 Policy Reconsidered." *Jerusalem Quarterly* (Israel), (3), 1977: 124–144.

704. Shamir, Shimon. *Self-views in Historical Perspective in Egypt and Israel: Proceedings of an Israeli-Egyptian Colloquium Held at the Tel-Aviv University*, April 15, 1980. Tel Aviv, Israel: Tel Aviv University, 1981. 132.

705. Shukr, Abdel Ghaffar, *Filastin fi fikr Abd al-Nasir: dirasah watha'i-qiyah* (Nasser and Palestine). Cairo: Jumhuriyat Misr al-'Arabiyah: Dar al-Mawqif al-'Arabi, 1982. 87.

706. *U.S. News and World Report.* "If Khrushchev Tries to Bail out Nasser." Volume 56, May 25th 1964: 63+.

See also:

Roth, Stephen J. (editor). *The Impact of the Six-Day War: A Twenty-Year Assessment.* (no. 787).

XI. Declining Years and Death

After the 1967 Arab-Israeli War, Nasser's political career came under intolerable pressure. It appears that most of the non-Arab world held him personally responsible for Egypt's military defeat. There is indeed a great deal less research done on this part of his life than on the earlier years.

A. War

707. Bar-Siman-Tov, Yaacov. *The Israeli-Egyptian War of Attrition 1969–1970: A Case Study of Limited Local War.* New York: Columbia University Press, 1980. 428.

Egypt and Israel conducted a war of attrition after the ceasefire of 1967. This books considers this to have been a major confrontation and analyses it as such.

708. Bulloch, John. *The Making of a War: The Middle East from 1967 to 1973.* London: Longman, 1974. 220.

A description of the events between 1967 and 1973 showing the political struggles which contributed to the eventual Yom Kippur War of 1973. The work also analyses the inter-Arab relations during that period.

709. Farid, Abdel Majid. *Min muhadir ijtima' at Abd al-Nasir al-Arabiyah wa-al-dawliyah 1967–1970* (Nasser's Arab and National Meetings). Beirut: Muassasat al-Abhath al-Arabiyah, 1979. 306.

710. Heikal, Mohamed. *The Road to Ramadan.* London: Collins, 1975. 285.

Narrates the events leading up to the 1973 Yom Kippur War and Egypt's failure to regain its lost territories.

711. Rubenstein, Alvin Z. *Red Star on the Nile: The Soviet-Egyptian Influence Relationship Since the June War.* Princeton, New Jersey: Princeton University Press, 1977. 383.

Egyptian-Soviet relationships in the aftermath of the June 1967 Six-Day War.

712. Seale, Patrick. "How Nasser Turned Grief to Cheers." *Observer*, June 11th 1967: 11+.

B. Domestic Affairs

713. Berl, Emmanuel. *Nasser tel qu'on le loue* (Nasser as He May Be Hired). Paris: Gallimard, 1968. 159.

714. Cooper, Mark N. *The Transformation of Egypt.* London; Canberra: Croom Helm; Baltimore, Maryland: Johns Hopkins University Press,- 1982. 278.

Egypt's political economy after 1967 is analysed in depth culminating in Sadat's peace initiative.

715. Entelis, John P. "Nasser's Egypt: The Failure of Charismatic Leadership." *Orbis*, 18(2), 1974: 451-464.

716. al-Hakim, Tawfiq. *The Return of Consciousness.* Translated from Arabic by Winder, Bayly. London: Macmillan, 1985. 83.

A work that created a sensation in Sadat's Egypt in 1974. Its main claim was that the Egyptians had been duped by Nasser and his politics.

717. Listowel, Judith. "President Nasser and Egypt." *Listener*, May 25th 1967: 673+.

718. Little, Tom. "The Burden Nasser Couldn't Shed." *Observer*, June 11th 1967: 13+.

719. Mansfield, Peter. "Egypt's Ataturk." *New Statesman*, August 29th 1969: 271+.

720. Mansfield, Peter. "How Safe Is Nasser?" *New Statesman*, March 15th 1968: 327+.

721. Rutherford, Malcolm. "What Makes Gamal Abdel Run?" *Spectator*, May 26th 1967: 609+.

722. Sykes, John. *Down into Egypt: A Revolution Observed*. London: Hutchinson, 1969. 190.

A portrait of a society facing crisis after the 1967 defeat.

723. *U.S. News and World Report*. "Egyptians to Nasser: Make War or Make Peace or Get out!" Volume 66, March 24th 1969: 56+.

See also:

Elahwal, Abdel Karim Aly. *Leader Linked Societal Consciousness of Modernization: Egypt's Nasser, 1968–1972*. (no. 797).

C. Death

724. Crossman, R. H. S. "Gamal Abdel Nasser." *New Statesman*, October 2nd 1970: 402+.

725. Du Bois, David Graham. "The Death of Nasser." *Black Scholar*, 2 (10), 1971: 45–47.

726. Fahmi, Faruq. *Jamal Abd al-Nasir wa-lughz al-mawt? man qatala Abd al-Nasir?* (Gamal Abdel Nasser and the Riddle of His Death. Who Killed Abdel Nasser?). Cairo: Mu'assasat Amun, 1987. 275.

727. Jasim, Aziz al-Sayyid. *Maqtal Jamal Abd al-Nasir* (The Killing of Gamal Abdel Nasser). Baghdad: Jaridat al-Iraq, 1985. 280.

An interesting re-appraisal that sheds light on inter-Arab perceptions.

728. el-Sebai, Youssef (Editor-in-Chief). *Gamal Abdel Nasser: In Memoriam*. Afro-Asian People's Solidarity Organization, 1971.

An anthology of papers, research works and poems.

729. Zorza, Victor. "Russia's Man, but No Stooge." *Guardian*, September 29th 1970: 2+.

XII.   General Place in History

A. Nasser's Leadership

730. Atasi, Jamal. *Jamal Abd al-Nasir wa-al-tajribah al-thawriyah: itlalah 'ala fikrihi al-istiratiji wa-al-tarikhi* (Nasser and the Revolutionary Experiment: His Strategic and Historic Thinking). Cairo: Dar al-Mustaqbal al-Arabi, 1983. 103.

731. Awdah, Muhammad and Stephens, Robert Henry. *Hiwar hawla Abd al-Nasir* (Discussions on Nasser). Cairo: Jumhuriyat Misr al-Arabiyah: Dar al-Mawqif al-Arabi lil-Sihafah wa-al-Nashr wa-al-Tawzi', 1982. 111.

732. Baker, R. W. *Egypt's Uncertain Revolution under Nasser and Sadat.* Cambridge, Massachusetts: Harvard University Press, 1978. 290.

733. Baker, Raymond William. *Nasser's Egypt: Power, Ideology, and Political Development.* Ph.D. Harvard University, 1972.

734. Beeson, Irene. "The 'Nasserization' of Egypt and Its Reversal under Sadat." *International Perspectives* (Canada), (4), 1975: 23–28.

735. Beliaev, I. P. and Primakov, E. M. *Egipet: vremia prezidenta Nasera* (Egypt in the Time of Nasser). Moscow: Mysl', 1981. 367.

736. Crabbs, Jack Jr. "Politics, History, and Culture in Nasser's Egypt." *International Journal of Middle East Studies* (Great Britain), 6 (4), 1975: 386–420.

Discusses the Nasser régime's attempts to rewrite history.

737. Dawud, Diya' al-Din. *Sanawat ma'a Abd al-Nasir* (Years with Abdel Nasser). Cairo: Dar al-Mawqif al-Arabi, 1984. 223.

738. Dekmejian, Hrair. *Egypt under Nasir: A Study in Political Dynamics*. London: University of London Press, 1972. 368. Albany: State University of New York Press, 1971.

A very good piece of political analysis showing Nasser interacting with the political environment that surrounded him in the fifties and sixties.

739. Fahmi, Faruq. *Haykal wa Abd al-Nasir* (Heikal and Abdel Nasser). Cairo: Mu'assasat Amun, 1987. 275.

Heikal was very close to Nasser both as a friend and as an adviser. He edited Al-Ahram daily and later became Minister of Information.

740. Farid, Abdel Majid. Arab Papers, number 8 Research Paper Series. *Nasser: A Reassessment*. London: Arab Research Centre, 1981. 32.

An Arab's assessment of Nasser. The work contains fifteen pages in Arabic.

741. Flower, Raymond. *Napoleon to Nasser: The Story of Modern Egypt*. London: Tom Stacey, 1972. 271.

A history of modern Egypt showing how Nasser tried to build an independent Egypt free of any foreign influence.

742. Hamrush, Ahmad. *Mujtama' Jamal Abd al-Nasir* (Nasser's Society). Cairo: Maktabat Madbuli, 1984. 302.

743. Imam, Abd Allah. *Nasir wa-Amir* (Nasser and Amer). Cairo: Mu'assasat Ruz al-Yusuf, 1985. 241.

Nasser's relationship with Amer defies political analysis for even after the debacle of 1956 and the rupture with Syria (both partly caused by Amer), Nasser retained—indeed promoted—Amer.

744. Kazim, Safinaz. *al-Khadi'ah al-Nasiriyah* (The Nasserist Trick). Cairo: Dar al-I'tisam, 1984. 100.

Based on "secret" Egyptian documents and an eyewitness account.

745. Khawaja, Sarfaz Hussain. *Nasser: A Soldier among Diplomats*. Progressive Series, 29. Lahore: Progressive Publishers, 1975. 67.

746. Lacouture, Jean. *The Demigods: Charismatic Leadership in the Third World.* Translated from the French *Quatre Hommes et Leurs Peuples* (Paris: Éditions du Seuil, 1969) by Wolf, Patricia. New York: Knopf; London: Secker and Warburg, 1970. 300.

A work that analyses four charismatic leaders: Nasser, Sihanouk, Nkrumah and Bourguiba. Written by the author of one of the most useful biographies on Nasser (see number 332 above).

747. Migdal, Joel S. "Vision and Practice: The Leader, The State, and The Transformation of Society." *International Political Science Review*, volume 9, issue 1, January 1988: 23–41.

An analysis of visionary leadership and its implementation of fundamental change. The author uses Egypt's Nasser, Mexico's Cardenas and Israel's Ben-Gurion as examples.

748. Morris, James. "President Nasser; The Man and His Vision." *Listener*, September 6th 1956: 329+.

749. Sadat, Anwar. *In Search of Identity.* London: Collins, 1978. 343.

An autobiography by Nasser's successor and one of the Free Officers.

750. Salim, Muhammad al-Sayyid. *al-Tahlil al-siyasi al-Nasiri: dirasah fi al-'aqa'id wa-al-siyasah* (An Investigation into Nasserist Politics: A Study of Beliefs and Politics). Beirut: Markaz Dirasat al-Wahda al-'Arabiyah, 1983. 395.

751. Springborg, Robert. "Patrimonialism and Policy Making in Egypt: Nasser and Sadat and the Tenure Policy for Reclaimed Lands." *Middle Eastern Studies* (Great Britain), 15 (1), 1979: 49–69.

A comparative study of political leadership in Egypt.

752. Steed, R. H. C. "Nasser the Opportunist." *Daily Telegraph*, July 23rd 1970: 14+.

753. Stephens, Robert. "Makers of the 20th Century: Nasser." *History Today*, volume 31, February 1981: 17+.

754. Stephens, Robert. "Nasser." *Observer*, October 4th 1970: 9+.

755. Tibah, Mustafa. *Hal inhara al-mashru' al-qawmi al-Nasiri! ru'yah jadidah lil-Nasiriyah* (Has the National Nasserist Plan Failed? New

Views on Nasserism). Cairo: al-Markaz al-Misri al-Arabi, 1986.
141.

756. Vaucher, Georges. *Gamal Abdul Nasser et Son Équipe* (Nasser and His Team). Paris: Juillard, 1959. Two volumes.

See also Chapter III, on general biographies of Nasser.

B. Egypt

757. Ansari, Hamid. *Egypt, The Stalled Society*. Albany, New York: State University of New York Press, 1986. 308.

Examining the shift from Nasser's secular ideas of Pan-Arabism and socialism to Sadat's open-door policy.

758. Ayubi, Nazih N. M. *Bureaucracy and Politics in Contemporary Egypt*. London: Ithaca Press, 1980. 547.

Analyses Nasser's attempts to transform Egypt's bureaucracy with the creation of a new bureaucratic politics.

759. Ben-Dor, Gabriel. "Stateness and Ideology in Contemporary Egyptian Politics." *Islam, Nationalism and Radicalism in Egypt and the Sudan*. Edited by Warburg, Gabriel R. and Kupferschmidt, Uri M. New York: Praeger, 1983: 73–96.

A comparative analysis of the political ideology in Egyptian society and the actual political situation that existed in the last thirty years.

760. Bianchi, Robert. "The Corporatization of the Egyptian Labor movement." *Middle East Journal*, volume 40, issue 3, Summer 1986: 429–444.

An exploration of government manipulation of the labour force under Nasser, Sadat and Mubarak.

761. Cooper, Mark N. "The Demilitarization of the Egyptian Cabinet." *International Journal of Middle East Studies*, volume 14, number 2, May 1982: 203–25.

An examination of the process of political liberalization from 1952 onwards. The conclusion reached is that today's Egypt has not achieved the stability desired despite the lowering of the military in the cabinet from 65 percent under Nasser to its current 9 percent.

762. Dessouki, Ali E. Hillal. *Democracy in Egypt: Problems and Prospects*. Cairo: American University in Cairo, 1978. 90.

Although dealing with post-Nasserist Egypt, this monograph contains several documents relating to parliamentary life in Egypt from 1952 onwards.

763. Girgis, Maurice. *Industrialization and Trade Patterns in Egypt*. Tubingen, F.R.G.: Mohr, 1977. 247.

A review of Egypt's public sector from 1950 to 1970 with the changing pattern of foreign trade and Egypt's poor export performance.

764. Harik, Iliya. "Continuity and Change in Local Development Policies in Egypt: From Nasser to Sadat." *International Journal of Middle East Studies*, volume 16, issue 1, March 1984: 43–66.

765. Harik, Iliya. "The Egypt of Nasser and Sadat: The Political Economy of Two Régimes." *American Historical Review*, volume 89, October 1984: 1127+.

Book reviews on John Waterbury's work on the two subjects (see number 781 below).

766. Harik, Iliya. *The Political Mobilization of Peasants: A Study of an Egyptian Community*. Bloomington, Indiana: Indiana University Press, 1974. 291.

A study of a small village in the Beheira Province illustrating the villagers' response to the revolution and the local political structures.

767. Haykal, Muhammad Hasanayn. *Li-Misr... la li-Abd al-Nasr* (For Egypt... Not for Abdel Nasser). Cairo: Markaz al-Ahram lil-Tarjamah wa-al-Nashr, Mu'assasat al-Ahram, 1987. 166.

768. Hopkins, Harry. *Egypt—The Crucible: The Unfinished Revolution of the Arab World*. London: Secker & Warburg, 1969. 513.

769. Hopwood, Derek. *Egypt: Politics and Society 1945–1984*. London; Boston, Massachusetts: Allen & Unwin, 1985. 203.

A fairly comprehensive survey of Egyptian life including Nasser's political ideology, Egypt's economic problems and the general cultural life of the country under him and Sadat. Interesting for its portrayal of the ordinary Egyptian's aspirations and hopes under Nasser.

770. Hussein, Mahmoud. *L'Égypte: lutte de classes et liberation natio-nale* (Egypt: the Class War and National Liberation). Paris: Petite collections Maspero 141, 1975. Two volumes.

Volume one covers Egyptian politics from 1945 to 1967. Volume two covers 1967–1973.

771. Issawi, Charles. *Egypt in Revolution: an Economic Analysis.* Oxford: Oxford University Press, 1963.

A study of Egypt's economic problems under Nasser. Issawi's approach is to define and list the problems of developments, e.g., urbanization, overpopulation, overexpenditure on arms, rate of economic growth, etc. This thesis directly relates Egypt's problems with her foreign policy since foreign aid becomes paramount.

772. Marsot, Afaf Lutfi al-Sayyid. *Protest Movements and Religious Undercurrents in Egypt: Past and Present.* Washington, D.C.: Centre for Contemporary Arab Studies, Georgetown University, 1984. 10.

773. McDermott, Anthony. *Egypt from Nasser to Mubarak: a Flawed Revolution.* London: New York: Croom Helm, 1988. 311.

774. Moore, Clement Henry. "Authoritarian Politics in Unincorporated Society: The Case of Nasser's Egypt." *Comparative Politics*, 6 (2), 1974: 193–218.

775. Riad, Mahmoud. *The Struggle for Peace in the Middle East.* London: Quartet Books, 1981. 365.

Egypt's foreign minister under Nasser and secretary-general of the Arab League after 1972 relates the story of the Egyptian-Israeli conflict and the road to peace.

776. Salih, Amani. *al-Mashru' al-qawmi li-Thawrat Yuliyu* (The National Programme of the July Revolution). Cairo: al-Markaz al- 'Arabi lil-Bahth wa-al-Nashr, 1984. 330.

777. Salim, Jamal. *Tanzimat al-Sirriyah li-thawrat 23 Yuliyu* (Secret Arrangements for the July 23rd Revolution). Cairo: Maktabat Madbuli, 1982. 329.

778. Voll, Sarah P. "Egyptian Land Reclamation since the Revolution." *Middle East Journal*, volume 34, number 2, Spring 1980: 127–148.

Surveys the recent history raising doubts about the economic value of such undertakings.

779. Vatikiotis, P. J. (editor). *Egypt since the Revolution*. London: Allen and Unwin; New York: Praeger, 1968.

A collection of papers delivered at a conference held at the University of London covering the economic, political and cultural developments in Egypt since the revolution. Amongst others Malcolm Kerr's chapter discusses the relative weight of ideology and Egyptian national interest under Nasser.

780. Vatikiotis, P. J. *Nasser and His Generation*. London: Croom Helm, 1978. 369.

A political study of Nasser showing him as a representative of his own generation. The work covers developments in Egypt during Nasser's youth, the Free Officers' movement, the revolution and inter-Arab relations. Vatikiotis is able to explain why the Nasser phenomenon took place and how his political cameo influenced his people so much.

781. Waterbury, John. *The Egypt of Nasser and Sadat: the Political Economy of Two Regimes*. Princeton, New Jersey: Princeton University Press, 1983. 475.

Showing how, after thirty years of revolution, Egypt was still unable to achieve its economic goals because of inherent class constraints within Egypt and because of external pressures from the industrialized nations (see 761 above on a similar treatment of political liberalization).

C. The Middle East

782. Adams, Michael and Mayhew, Christopher. *Publish It Not... The Middle East Cover-Up*. London, 1975.

783. Badeau, John S. *The Middle East Remembered*. Washington, D.C.: Middle East Institute, 1982. 280.

As ambassador to Nasser's Egypt for a while, Badeau describes half a century of change in the Middle East.

784. Cantori, Louis J. and Harik, Iliya (editors). *Local Politics and Development in the Middle East*. Boulder, Colorado; London: Westview Press, 1984. 258.

785. Chevallier, Dominique (editor). *Renouvellements du monde arabe, 1952–1982: pensées politiques et confrontations internationales* (Renewal of the Arab World, 1952–1982: Political Thoughts and International Confrontations). Paris: Collection U., 1987. 229.

A collection dealing with Egypt's political developments under both Nasser and Sadat.

786. Hershlag, Z. Y. *Introduction to the Modern Economic History of the Middle East*. Leyden: Brill, 1964. 419.

The sections on Egypt deal with the diplomatic and political history and the economic problems during the first two decades of Nasser's life.

787. Roth, Stephen J. (editor). *The Impact of the Six-Day War: A Twenty-Year Assessment*. London: Macmillan Press (in association with the Institute of Jewish Affairs), 1988. 316.

788. Shwadran, B. "Oil and the Middle East Crisis." *International Journal*, 12 (1), 1956–1957: 13–23.

XIII.   Theses, Bibliographies and Reviews

A. Brief Biographical Entries

789. *Chambers Biographical Dictionary*. Edited by Thorne, J. O. and Collocott, T. C. Edinburgh: W. & R. Chambers Ltd., 1984. 975–976.

A brief summary of Nasser's life.

790. *Dictionary of World History*. Edited by Howat, G. M. D. 1047–1048. London: Nelson, 1973.

Factual summary of Nasser's life followed by an entry on 'Nasserism'.

791. *The International Who's Who 1970–71*. London: Europo Publications. 1151.

Very brief resumé of Nasser's career as an army officer and political leader.

792. *Keesing's Contemporary Archives 1969–1970*. Edited by Rosenberger, Walter and Tobin, Herbert C. London, Keesing's Publications Ltd., 1970. Volume 17. Entries may be found as follows:

- 24212 A: Non-aligned nations.
- 24225 A: Jordan.
- 24261 A: United Arab Republic.
- 24309 A: Syria.
- 23119 A: United Arab Republic.
- 23146 D: Syria.

- 23325 A: Middle East.
- 23421 A: Syria.
- 23520 A: Lebanon.
- 23683 A: Sudan.
- 23689 A: Islamic Summit Conference.
- 23704 A: Lebanon.

793. *The Macmillan Dictionary of Biography.* Edited by Jones, Barry and Dixon, M. V. London: Macmillan, 1981. 854.

B. Theses

In recent years there has been a renewed interest in scholarly research on Nasser. The following is only a small selection of significant works which, with the benefit of hindsight, illuminate a great deal of Nasser's life and political influence.

794. Abo-El-Enein, Mohammed Mahmoud. *The State, Dominant Class Segments, and Capital Accumulation in Egypt since 1805, with Special Reference to the "Open Door" Élite of 1974–1986.* Ph.D. Madison: The University of Wisconsin, 1989. 281. (Volume 50/10– A of *Dissertation Abstracts International*, page 3365).

An analysis of the production of capital in Egypt showing how, during the Nasser years, state capitalism produced a bureaucratic class that allied itself with the traditional bourgeoisie.

795. El-Ashram, Mohamed Abdel-Halim. *Nasser's Ideology and Organization: A Modernizing Experiment in Egypt, 1952–1970.* Ph.D. New York University, 1972. 408. (Volume 35/01-A of *Dissertation Abstracts International*, page 531).

796. Diandudi, Joncker K. Ibn. *A Review of Selected Materials on the Development Strategies of Zhou Enlai, Fidel Castro and Gamal Abdel Nasser.* Ph.D. The Ohio State University, 1984. 560. (Volume 54/06–A of *Dissertation Abstracts International*, page 1856).

The main argument is that a political leader's beliefs about relevant strategies and tactics to transform his society tend to impact on his country's foreign policy.

797. Elahwal, Abdel Karim Aly. *Leader Linked Societal Consciousness of Modernization: Egypt's Nasser, 1968–1972.* Ph.D. The Catholic University of America, 1973. 252. (Volume 33/12–A of *Dissertation Abstracts International,* page 7036).

798. Eldahry, Ahmed Kamal. *Budgeting and Policy Analysis: The Egyptian Case.* Ph.D. State University of New York at Binghamton, 1981. 167. (Volume 42/06–A of *Dissertation Abstracts International,* page 2852).

The relationship between public policy, the political system and other systematic variables reflected in the budget. The work covers pre-1952 Egypt and the Nasser-Sadat eras.

799. Eldahry, Ragaa Osman. *Comparative Labor Policy in Egypt.* Ph.D. State University of New York at Binghamton, 1987. 185. (Volume 48/02–A of *Dissertation Abstracts International,* page 478).

A comparative study of Nasser's and Sadat's labour policies. Under Nasser labour received substantial benefits in return for supporting the régime. Sadat's open door policy caused a decline in the labour force to the detriment of Egypt. Nasser's depoliticisation of labour is seen as economically successful.

800. Hamed, Osama Ahmad. *The State as an Agent of Economic Development: Egypt, 1952–1970.* Ph.D. University of California in Los Angeles, 1987. 134. (Volume 48/03–A of *Dissertation Abstracts International,* page 703).

Shows the gradual development of state control of the Egyptian economy. Despite an unwieldy bureaucracy Nasser managed some major economic transformation including an increase in per capita income and a substantial diversification of exports.

801. Harvey, Mark Kate McCarty. *The Political Views of Lenin and Nasser on State and Trans-State Politics: A Comparative Analysis.* Ph.D. University of Southern Mississippi, 1973. 161. (Volume 34/07–A of *Dissertation Abstracts International,* page 4364).

802. Hason, Sana. *Bureaucracy and Political Participation in 'Modern' Egypt.* Harvard University, 1984. 492. (Volume 45/07–A of *Dissertation Abstracts International,* page 2242).

803. Hosseinzadeh, Esmail. *An Evaluation of the Theory of Non-Capitalist Development: The Case of Nasser's Egypt.* Ph.D. New School

for Social Research, 1987. 311. (Volume 48/12–A of *Dissertation Abstracts International*, page 3171).

An intricately detailed study of the Soviet concept of "non-capitalism" as a first step towards socialism. It shows the concept to be flawed because Nasser's "non-capitalism" was a combination of policy justification and policy prescriptions.

804. Kamel, Ibrahim Ahmed. *The Impact of Nasser's Regime on Labor Relations in Egypt.* Ph.D. The University of Michigan, 1970. 236. (Volume 31/08–A of *Dissertation Abstracts International*, page 3711).

805. Mustafa, Muhammad Muhammad Hussein. *The Role of Cognitive Perceptions: Nasser and Sadat.* Ph.D. Boston University, 1985. 511. (Volume 46/11-A of *Dissertation Abstracts International*, page 3476).

An assessment of the role of leaders' perceptions of national identity in their foreign policy choices and decisions and the positive correlation between perception and practice.

806. Selim, Mohammed El-Sayed. *The Operational Code Belief System and Foreign Policy Decision Making: The Case of Gamal Abdel-Nasser.* Ph.D. Carlton University (Canada), 1979. (Volume 41/05–A of *Dissertation Abstracts International*, page 2280).

807. Shalabieh, Mahmoud Ibrahim. *A Comparison of Political Persuasion on Radio Cairo in the Eras of Nasser and Sadat.* Ohio State University, 1985. 303. (Available from University Microfilms International, Ann Arbor, Michigan, order number NBK 85–26247) Ph.D. The Ohio State University, 1985. 312. (Volume 46/09–A of *Dissertation Abstracts International*, page 2477).

An excellent study of Nasser's most potent weapon used to convert the masses to revolutionary ideas. Under Sadat support for his peace with Israel initiative was achieved using similar methods.

808. Sherif, Khaled Ahmed Fouad. *The Egyptian Pharmaceutical Industry, A Sector in Transition.* Ph.D. Boston University, 1986. 242. (Volume 47/03–A of *Dissertation Abstracts International*, page 1055).

Although specific to one industry, the work shows the long-term detrimental effect of Nasser's nationalisation process.

809. Souryal, Safwat Sabit. *Andrew Jackson and Gamal Abdul-Nasser: A Behavioral Study in Comparative Political Leadership.* Ph.D. The University of Utah, 1971. 361. (Volume 32/03–A of *Dissertation Abstracts International,* page 1592).

810. Zeidan, Shawky Saad. *The Emergence of Charisma: A Study of Nasser and Muhammad.* Ph.D. University of Colorado at Boulder, 1976. 413. (Volume 37/12–A of *Dissertation Abstracts International,* page 7950).

811. Yahya, Ali M. *Egypt and the Soviet Union, 1955–1972: A Study in the Power of the Small State.* Ph.D. Indiana University, 1981. 277. (Volume 41/12–A of *Dissertation Abstracts International,* page 5238).

See also:

Abbas, Jabir Ali. *Points of Departure in Egypt's Foreign Policy: The Essence of Nasser's Power.* (no. 604).

Baker, Raymond William. *Nasser's Egypt: Power, Ideology and Political Development.* (no. 733).

Beattie, Kirk James. *Egypt: The Struggle for Hegemony, 1952–1981.* (no. 579).

Bin Salamon, Ahmed S. *Reform of al-Azhar in the 20th Century.* (no. 341).

Botman, Selma. *Oppositional Politics in Egypt: The Communist Movement, 1939–1954.* (no. 394).

Burns, William J. *"The Carrot and the Stick": Economic Aid and American Policy Towards Egypt, 1955–1967.* (no. 407).

Fallatah, Mohammed A. S. *The Emergence of Pan-Arabism and Its Impact on Egyptian Foreign Policy: 1945–1981.* (no. 619).

Gordon, Joel S. *Towards Nasser's Egypt: The Consolidation of the July Revolution and the End of the Old Regime, 1952–1955.* (no. 384).

Hall, Donna Jean. *The Political Agenda of the Palestine Liberation Organisation.* (no. 687).

Hasour, Tawfiq Yousef. *The Arab League in Egyptian Foreign Policy under Gamal Abdel-Nasser: A Study of International Regional Organization in the Foreign Policy of Small State. (no. 626).*

Ismail, Mahmoud Ismail Mohamed. *Nationalism in Egypt before Nasser's Revolution.* (no. 353).

Al-Jebarin, Abdulqadir Ismail. *The United States-Egyptian Relations, 1945–1958.* (no. 417).

Nash, Marguerite Bou-Raad. *National Interest and Neutralism in Nasser's Foreign Policy: Three Case Studies.* (no. 563).

Al-Solami, Dawi Awaad. *British Preparations for the Suez War.* (no. 475).

Shafik, Fouad Fahmy. *The Press and Politics of Modern Egypt: 1798–1970. A Comparative Analysis of Causal Relationships.* (no. 362).

Whittington, Dale. *Water Management in Egypt: A Case Study of the Aswan High Dam.* (no. 371).

C. Bibliographies and Reviews

Almost every bibliographical or major reference work has a section on Nasser. Other generic entries mentioned elsewhere in this work may also prove useful, e.g., Non-alignment/Neutralism, Arab-Israeli conflict, Egypt/ United Arab Republic, etc.

812. Badeau, John S. "Nasser." *Worldview*, 16 (3), 1973: 28–31.

    Review article on works by Heikal, Stephens and Nutting.

813. Blake, G. H. and Swearingen, W. D. (editors). *The Suez Canal: A Commemorative Bibliography 1975*. University of Durham Occasional Papers Series, number 4, 1975. Centre for Middle Eastern and Islamic Studies, 1975. 49.

814. Makar, Ragi N. *Egypt.* World Bibliographical Series, volume 86, Oxford; Santa Barbara: 1988. 306.

815. Springborg, Robert. "In search of Egypt." *Politics* (Australia), 11 (1), 1976: 85–89.

    A review of works on Nasser and Egypt by Dekmejian, Harik, Mayfield and Perlmutter.

816. Zaki, A. "A Bibliography of the Suez Canal 1869–1969." *Bulletin de la Société de Geographie d'Égypte*, 40, 1967: 237–244.

817. Zamora, Marion D. and Deane, Glenn D. "Nasser and His Generation." *Annals of the American Academy of Political and Social Science*, volume 446, November 1979: 179+.

A book review of P. J. Vatikiotis's work of the same title (see number 780 above).

818. Ziring, Laurence. *The Middle East Political Dictionary*. Santa Barbara, California; Oxford, England: ABC-CLIO Information Services, 1984. 416.

Over thirty entries on Egypt under such headings as British occupation, Camp David, A.S.U. (Arab Socialist Union).

Serial Publications Cited

This is an alphabetical list of all serial publications that appear in the bibliography including periodicals and newspapers. Numbers refer to entries, not pages.

African Affairs, 646
Ahram, Al, 31
Akhbar, Al, 32
American Foreign Policy: Current
  Documents, 7
American Historical Review, 765
American Journal of International
  Law, 512, 532
Annals of the American Academy of
  Political and Social Science, 817
Année Politique et Économique, L',
  548
Annuaire Francais de Droit Interna-
  tional, 473
Annual Survey of American Law, 472
Arab Chronicle, The, 33
Arab Observer, The, 34
Arab Report and Record, 35
Arab World, The, 36
Archiv Orientalni, 647
Asian Affairs, 37

Black Scholar, 725

Bulletin de la Société de Geographie
  d'Égypte, 816
Business Week, 38, 39

Cahiers de l'Europe Naissante, Les,
  515
Cahiers de l'Orient Contemporain,
  Les, 40, 492
Capital, 561
Christian Century, 587
Chronology of Arab Politics, 41
Commentary, 42, 486, 639
Comparative Politics, 774
Comptes Rendus, Académie de Sci-
  ences Coloniales, 552
Comptes Rendus, Académie des Sci-
  ences Morales et Politiques, 453
Congressional Quarterly Almanac, 1
Contemporary Review, 340

Dacca University Studies, 606
Daily Star, 43

Author Index

Authors' names are arranged alphabetically ignoring the Arabic definite articles 'el' or 'al' that prefix many surnames. Numbers refer to entries, not pages.

Subject Index

Numbers refer to entries, not pages.

About the Author

FAYSAL MIKDADI is an adviser to the Wiltshire County Council in England. A freelance journalist and author, he earlier published *Chateaux en Palestine*, *A Return: The Siege of Beirut*, and *Tamra*.